Thomas Wentworth Higginson

The new world and the new book

an address, delivered before the Nineteenth century club of New York city, Jan. 15,

1891

Thomas Wentworth Higginson

The new world and the new book
an address, delivered before the Nineteenth century club of New York city, Jan. 15, 1891

ISBN/EAN: 9783743308886

Manufactured in Europe, USA, Canada, Australia, Japa

Cover: Foto ©Thomas Meinert / pixelio.de

Manufactured and distributed by brebook publishing software (www.brebook.com)

Thomas Wentworth Higginson

The new world and the new book

THE NEW WORLD AND THE NEW BOOK

An Address

DELIVERED BEFORE THE NINETEENTH CENTURY CLUB OF NEW
YORK CITY, JAN. 15, 1891

WITH KINDRED ESSAYS

BY

THOMAS WENTWORTH HIGGINSON

———

BOSTON
LEE AND SHEPARD PUBLISHERS
1892

TYPOGRAPHY AND ELECTROTYPING BY
C. J. PETERS & SON, BOSTON.

PREFACE

THE address which forms the first chapter in these pages was given originally before the Nineteenth Century Club of New York City on January 15, 1891, and was written out afterward. Its title was suggested by that of a remarkable essay contributed many years ago to the *Atlantic Monthly*, by my friend David Atwood Wasson and entitled, " The New World and the New Man." I am indebted to the proprietors of the *Century*, the *Independent*, the *Christian Union*, and *Harper's Bazar* for permission to reprint such of the remaining chapters as appeared in their respective columns.

Nothing is farther from the present writer's wish than to pander to any petty national vanity, his sole desire being to assist in creating a modest and reasonable self-respect. The civil war bequeathed to us Americans, twenty-five

years ago, a great revival of national feeling;
but this has been followed in some quarters,
during the last few years, by a curious relapse
into something of the old colonial and apologetic attitude; enhanced, no doubt, by the
vexations and humiliations of the long struggle
for international copyright. This is the frame
of mind which is deprecated in this volume,
because it is the last source from which any
strong or self-reliant literary work can proceed.
In the words of Thoreau, "I do not propose to
write an ode to dejection, but to brag as lustily
as chanticleer in the morning, standing on his
roost, if only to wake my neighbors up."

CAMBRIDGE, MASS., October 1, 1891.

CONTENTS

CONTENTS

THE NEW WORLD AND THE NEW BOOK

[AN ADDRESS DELIVERED BEFORE THE "NINETEENTH CENTURY CLUB," JANUARY 15, 1891.]

IT is a remarkable fact that the man who has, among all American authors, made the most daring and almost revolutionary claims in behalf of American literature should yet have been, among all these authors, the most equable in temperament and the most cosmopolitan in training.

Washington Irving was, as one may say, born a citizen of the world, for he was born in New York City. He was not a rustic nor a Puritan, nor even, in the American sense, a Yankee. He spent twenty-one years of his life in foreign countries. He was mistaken in England for an English writer. He was accepted as an adopted Spaniard in Spain. He

died before the outbreak of the great Civil
War, which did so much to convince us, for a
time at least, that we were a nation. Yet it
was Washington Irving who wrote to John
Lothrop Motley, in 1857, two years before his
own death : —

" You are properly sensible of the high calling of the American press, that rising tribunal
before which the history of all nations is to be
revised and rewritten, and the judgment of past
ages to be corrected or confirmed." [1]

The utmost claim of the most impassioned
Fourth of July orator has never involved any
declaration of literary independence to be compared with this deliberate utterance of the
placid and world-experienced Irving. It was
the fashion of earlier critics to pity him for having been born into a country without a past.
This passage showed him to have rejoiced in
being born into a country with a future. His
" broad and eclectic genius," as Warner well
calls it, was surely not given to bragging or
to vagueness. He must have meant something
by this daring statement. What did he mean ?

[1] July 17, 1857. Motley Correspondence, i. 203.

There are some things which it is very certain that he did not mean. He certainly did not accept the Matthew Arnold attitude, that to talk of a distinctive American press at all is an absurdity. Arnold finds material for profound ridicule in the fact that there exists a "Primer of American Literature;" this poor little Cinderella, cut off from all schooling, must not even have a primer of her own. Irving certainly did not assume the Goldwin Smith attitude, that this nation is itself but a schism, and should be viewed accordingly; as if one should talk of there being only a schism between an oak-tree and its seedling, and should try to correct the unhappy separation by trowel and gardener's wax. He certainly did not accept the theory sometimes so earnestly advocated among us, of a "cosmopolitan tribunal," which always turns out to mean a tribunal where all other nations are to be admitted to the jury-box, while America is to get no farther than the prisoners' dock. Irving would have made as short work with such a cosmopolitan tribunal as did Alice in Wonderland with the jury-box of small quadrupeds, when she refused to obey the king's order that all persons over a mile high should leave the court-room. In truth, the tone of Irving's remark carries us back, by its audacious self-reliance, to the answer said to have been given by the Delphic oracle to Cicero in his youth. It told him, according to Plutarch, to live for himself, and not to take the opinions of others for his guide; and the German Niebuhr thinks that "if the answer was really given, it might well tempt us to believe in the actual inspiration of the priestess." [1]

At any rate, Irving must have meant something by the remark. What could he have meant? What is this touchstone that the American press must apply to the history and the thought of the world? The touchstone, I should unhesitatingly reply, of the Declaration of Independence; or rather, perhaps, of those five opening words into which the essence of the Declaration of Independence was concentrated; the five words within which, as Lincoln said, Jefferson embodied an eternal truth. "All men are created equal;"—that is, equally men, and each entitled to be counted and considered as an individual.

[1] Hist. of Rome, tr. by Schmitz, v. 35.

From this simple assumption flowed all that is distinctive in American society. From it resulted, as a political inference, universal suffrage; that is, a suffrage constantly tending to be universal, although it still leaves out one-half the human race. This universal suffrage is inevitably based on the doctrine of human equality, as further interpreted by Franklin's remark that the poor man has an equal right to the suffrage with the rich man, "and more need," because he has fewer ways in which to protect himself. But it is not true, as even such acute European observers as M. Scherer and Sir Henry Maine assume, that "democracy is but a form of government;" for democracy has just as distinct a place in society, and, above all, in the realm of literature. The touchstone there applied is just the same, and it consists in the essential dignity and value of the individual man. The distinctive attitude of the American press must lie, if anywhere, in its recognition of this individual importance and worth.

The five words of Jefferson — words which Matthew Arnold pronounced "not solid," thus prove themselves solid enough to sustain not merely the government of sixty-three million people, but their literature. Instead of avoiding, with Goethe, the common, *das Gemeinde*, American literature must freely seek the common; its fiction must record not queens and Cleopatras alone, but the emotion in the heart of the schoolgirl and the sempstress; its history must record, not great generals alone, but the nameless boys whose graves people with undying memories every soldiers' cemetery from Arlington to Chattanooga.

And Motley the pupil was not unworthy of Irving from whom the suggestion came. His "Dutch Republic" was written in this American spirit. William the Silent remains in our memory as no more essentially a hero than John Haring, who held single-handed his submerged dike against an army; and Philip of Burgundy and his knights of the Golden Fleece are painted as far less important than John Coster, the Antwerp apothecary, printing his little grammar with movable types. Motley wrote from England, in the midst of an intoxicating social success, that he never should wish America

" to be Anglicized in the aristocratic sense " of
the term;[1] and he described the beautiful
English country-seats as "paradises very per-
verting to the moral and politico-economical
sense," and sure to "pass away, one of these
centuries, in the general progress of humanity."[2]
And he afterwards said the profoundest thing
ever uttered in regard to our Civil War, when
he said that it was not, in the ordinary sense, " a
military war," but a contest of two principles.[3]
Wendell Phillips once told me that as the anti-
slavery contest made him an American, so
Europe made Motley one; and when the two
young aristocrats met after years of absence,
they both found that they had thus experienced
religion.

When we pass to other great American
authors, we see that Emerson lifted his voice
and spoke even to the humblest of the people
of the intrinsic dignity of man : —

> God said, I am tired of kings,
>   I suffer them no more ;
> Up to my ear each morning brings
>   The outrage of the poor.

[1] Corresp. ii. 294.   [2] *Ibid.* ii. 280.   [3] *Ibid.* ii. 82.

I will have never a noble,
  No lineage counted great;
Fishers and choppers and ploughmen
  Shall constitute a State.

. . . .

To-day unbind the captive,
  So only are ye unbound :
Lift up a people from the dust,
  Trump of their freedom, sound !

Pay ransom to the owner,
  And fill the bag to the brim :
Who is the owner ? The slave is owner,
  And ever was. Pay him.

That poem was not written for a few cultivated people only. I heard it read to an armed
regiment of freed slaves, standing silent with
dusky faces, with the solemn arches of the live
oaks above them, each tree draped with long
festoons of gray moss across its hundred feet of
shade. And never reader had an audience more
serious, more thoughtful. The words which to
others are literature, to them were life.

And all of that early transcendental school
which did so much to emancipate and national-
ize American literature, did it by recognizing
this same fact. From the depth of their so-called
idealism they recognized the infinite value of

the individual man. Thoreau, who has been so
incorrectly and even cruelly described as a man
who spurned his fellows, wrote that noble
sentence, forever refuting such critics, " What is
nature, without a human life passing within
her? Many joys and many sorrows are the
lights and shadows in which she shines most
beautiful." Hawthorne came nearest to a
portrayal of himself in that exquisite prose-
poem of " The Threefold Destiny," in which the
world-weary man returns to his native village
and finds all his early dreams fulfilled in the life
beside his own hearthstone. Margaret Fuller
Ossoli wrote the profoundest phrase of criticism
which has yet proceeded from any American
critic, when she said that in a work of fiction
we need to hear the excuses that men make to
themselves for their worthlessness.

And now that this early ideal movement has
passed by, the far wider movement which is
establishing American fiction, not in one local-
ity alone, but on a field broad as the continent,
unconsciously recognizes this one principle, —
the essential dignity and worth of the individual man. This is what enables it to dispense

with the toy of royalty and the mechanism of separate classes, and to reach human nature itself. When we look at the masters of English fiction, Scott and Jane Austen, we notice that in scarcely one of their novels does one person ever swerve on the closing page from the precise social position he has held from the beginning. Society in their hands is fixed, not fluid. Of course, there are a few concealed heirs, a few revealed strawberry leaves, but never any essential change. I can recall no real social promotion in all the Waverley novels except where Halbert Glendinning weds the maid of Avenel, and there the tutelary genius disappears singing, —

"The churl is lord, the maid is bride," —

and it proved necessary for Scott to write a sequel, explaining that the marriage was on the whole a rather unhappy one, and that luckily they had no children. Not that Scott did not appreciate with the keenest zest his own Jeannie Deanses and Dandie Dinmonts, but they must keep their place ; it is not human nature they vindicate, but peasant virtues.

But from the moment American fiction came upon the scene, it brought a change. Peasant virtue vanishes when the peasant is a possible president, and what takes its place is individual manhood, irrespective of social position. The heroes who successively conquered Europe in the hands of American authors were of low estate, — a backwoodsman, a pilot, a negro slave, a lamplighter; to which gallery Bret Harte added the gambler, and the authors of " Democracy " and the " Bread-Winners " flung in the politician. In all these figures social distinctions disappear : " a man's a man for a' that." And so of our later writers, Miss Wilkins in New England, Miss Murfree in Tennessee, Mr. Cable in Louisiana, Mr. Howe in Kansas, Dr. Eggleston in Indiana, Julien Gordon in New York, all represent the same impulse ; all recognize that " all men are created equal " in Jefferson's sense, because all recognize the essential and inalienable value of the individual man.

It would be, of course, absurd to claim that America represents the whole of this tendency. for the tendency is a part of that wave of democratic feeling which is overflowing the world.

But Dickens, who initiated the movement in English fiction, was unquestionably influenced by that very American life which he disliked and caricatured, and we have since seen a similar impulse spread through other countries. In the Russian, the Norwegian, the Spanish, the Italian fiction, we now rarely find a plot turning on some merely conventional difference between the social positions of hero and heroine. In England the change has been made more slowly than elsewhere, so incongruous is it in the midst of a society which still, in the phrase of Brander Matthews, accepts dukes. Indeed, it is curious to observe that for a time it was still found necessary, in the earlier stages of the transition, to label the hero with his precise social position; — as, " Steven Lawrence, Yeoman," " John Halifax, Gentleman," — whereas in America it would have been left for the reader to find out whether John Halifax was or was not a gentleman, and no label would have been thought needful.

And I hasten to add, what I should not always have felt justified in saying, that this American tendency comes to its highest point and is best indicated in the later work of Mr. Howells. Happy is that author whose final admirers are, as heroes used to say, " the captives of his bow and spear," the men from whom he met his earlier criticism.   Happy is that man who has the patience to follow, like Cicero, his own genius, and not to take the opinions of others for his guide.   And the earlier work of Mr. Howells — that is, everything before " The Rise of Silas Lapham," " Annie Kilburn," and " The Hazard of New Fortunes " — falls now into its right place ; its alleged thinness becomes merely that of the painter's sketches and studies before his maturer work begins.   As the Emperor Alaric felt always an unseen power drawing him on to Rome, so Howells has evidently felt a magnet drawing him on to New York, and it was not until he set up his canvas there that it had due proportions.   My friend Mr. James Parton used to say that students must live in New England, where there were better libraries, but that " loafers and men of genius " should live in New York.   To me personally it seems a high price to pay for the privileges either of genius or of loafing, but it is well that Howells has at last paid it for the sake of the results. It is impossible to deny that he as a critic has proved himself sometimes narrow, and has rejected with too great vehemence that which lay outside of his especial domain. It is not necessary, because one prefers apples, to condemn oranges; and he has sometimes needed the caution of the old judge to the young one: " Beware how you give reasons for your decisions; for, while your decisions will usually be right, your reasons will very often be wrong." But as he has become touched more and more with the enthusiasm of humanity, he has grown better than his reasons, far better than his criticisms; and it is with him and with the school he represents that the hope of American literature just now rests. The reason why he finds no delicate shading or gradation of character unimportant is that he represents the dignity and importance of the individual man.

When the future literary historian of the English-speaking world looks back to this period he will be compelled to say, " While England hailed as great writing and significant additions to literature the brutalities of Haggard and the garlic flavors of Kipling, there was in America a student of life, who painted with the skill that Scott revered in Miss Austen, but not on the two inches of ivory that Miss Austen chose. He painted on a canvas large enough for the tragedies of New York, large enough for the future of America. Rich and luminous as George Eliot, he had the sense of form and symmetry which she had not; graphic in his characterization as Hardy, he did not stop, like Hardy, with a single circle of villagers. What the future critic will say, we too should be ready to perceive. If England finds him tiresome, so much the worse for England; if England prefers dime novels and cut-and-thrust Christmas melodramas, and finds in what Howells writes only "transatlantic kickshaws" because he paints character and life, we must say, as our fathers did, "Farewell, dear England," and seek what is our own. Emerson set free our poetry, our prose; Howells is setting free our fiction; he himself is as yet only half out of the chrysalis, but the wings are there.

It must always be remembered that in literature, alone of all arts, place is of secondary importance, for its masterpieces can be carried round the world in one's pockets. We need to go to Europe to see the great galleries, to hear the music of Wagner, but the boy who reads Æschylus and Horace and Shakespeare by his pine-knot fire has at his command the essence of all universities, so far as literary training goes. But were this otherwise, we must remember that libraries, galleries, and buildings are all secondary to that great human life of which they are only the secretions or appendages. "My Madonnas" — thus wrote to me that recluse woman of genius, Emily Dickinson — "are the women who pass my house to their work, bearing Saviours in their arms." Words wait on thoughts, thoughts on life; and after these, technical training is an easy thing. "The *art* of composition," wrote Thoreau, "is as simple as the discharge of a bullet from a rifle, and its masterpieces imply an infinitely greater force behind them." What are the two unmistakable rifle-shots in American literature thus far? John Brown's speech in the court-room and Lincoln's Gettysburg address.

Yielding to no one in the desire to see our

land filled with libraries, with galleries, with museums, with fine buildings, I must still maintain that all those things are secondary to that vigorous American life, which is destined to assimilate and digest them all. We are still in allegiance to Europe for a thousand things; — clothes, art, scholarship. For many years we must yet go to Europe as did Robinson Crusoe to his wreck, for the very materials of living. But materials take their value from him who uses them, and that wreck would have long since passed from memory had there not been a Robinson Crusoe. I am willing to be censured for too much national self-confidence, for it is still true that we, like the young Cicero, need that quality. Goethe's world-literature is, no doubt, the ultimate aim, but a strong national literature must come first. The new book must express the spirit of the New World. We need some repressing, no doubt, and every European newspaper is free to apply it; we listen with exemplary meekness to every little European lecturer who comes to enlighten us, in words of one syllable, as to what we knew very well before. We need something of repression, but

much more of stimulus. So Spenser's Brito-
mart, when she entered the enchanted hall,
found above four doors in succession the
inscription, "Be bold! be bold! be bold! be
bold!" and only over the fifth door was the
inscription, needful but wholly subordinate,
"Be not too bold!"

II

AN AMERICAN TEMPERAMENT

THE recent assertion of the London correspondent of the New York *Tribune*, that Englishmen like every American to be an American, has a curious interest in connection with some remarks of the late Matthew Arnold, which seem to look in an opposite direction. Lord Houghton once told me that the earlier American guests in London society were often censured as being too English in appearance and manner, and as wanting in a distinctive flavor of Americanism. He instanced Ticknor and Sumner; and we can all remember that there were at first similar criticisms on Lowell. It is indeed a form of comment to which all Americans are subject in England, if they have the ·ill-luck to have color in their cheeks and not to speak very much through their noses; in that case they are apt to pass for Englishmen by no wish of their own, and to be suspected of a little double dealing when they hasten to reveal their birthplace. It very often turns out that the demand for a distinctive Americanism really seeks only the external peculiarities that made Joaquin Miller and Buffalo Bill popular; an Americanism that can at any moment be annihilated by a pair of scissors. It is something, no doubt, to be allowed even such an amount of nationality as this; and Washington Irving attributed the English curiosity about him to the fact that he held a quill in his fingers instead of sticking it in his hair, as was expected.

But it would seem that Mr. Arnold, on the other hand, disapproved the attempt to set up any claim whatever to a distinctive American temperament; and he has twice held up one of our own authors for reprobation as having asserted that the American is, on the whole, of lighter build and has " a drop more of nervous fluid " than the Englishman. This is not the way, he thinks, in which a serious literature is to be formed. But it turns out that the immediate object of the writer of the objectionable remark was not to found a literature, but simply to utter a physiological caution ; the object of the essay in which it occurs — one called "The Murder of the Innocents,"[1] being simply to caution this more nervous race against overworking their children in school; an aim which was certainly as far as possible from what Mr. Arnold calls "tall talk and self-glorification." If a nation is not to be saved by pointing out is own physiological perils, what is to save it?

As a matter of fact, it will be generally claimed by Americans, I fancy, that whatever else their much-discussed nation may have, it has at least developed a temperament for itself; "an ill-favored thing, but mine own," as Touchstone says of Audrey. There is no vanity or self-assertion involved in this, any more than when a person of blond complexion claims not to be a brunette or a brunette meekly insists upon not being regarded as fair-haired. If the American is expected to be in all respects the duplicate of the Englishman, and is only charged with inexpressible inferiority in quality and size, let us know it; but if two hundred and fifty years of transplantation under a new sky and in new conditions have made any difference

[1] Out-Door Papers, p. 104.

in the type, let us know that also. In truth, the difference is already so marked that Mr. Arnold himself concedes it at every step in his argument, and has indeed stated it in very much the same terms which an American would have employed. In a paper entitled "From Easter to August,"[1] he says frankly: "Our countrymen [namely, the English], with a thousand good qualities, are really perhaps a good deal wanting in lucidity and flexibility;" and again in the same essay : "The whole American nation may be called intelligent; that is, quick." This would seem to be conceding the very point at issue between himself and the American writer whom he is criticising.

The same difference of temperament, in the direction of a greater quickness — what the wit of Edmund Quincy once designated as "specific levity" — on the part of Americans is certainly very apparent to every one of us who visits England; and not infrequently makes itself perceptible, even without a surgical operation, to our English visitors. Professor Tyndall is reported to have said — and if he did not say it,

---

[1] *Nineteenth Century* for September, 1887.

some one else pointed it out for him — that,
whereas in his London scientific lectures he
always had to repeat his explanations three
times; first telling his audience in advance
what his experiments were to accomplish, then
during the process explaining what was being
accomplished, and then at last recapitulating
what had actually been done ; he found it best,
in America, to omit one, if not two, of these
expositions. In much the same way, the director
of a company of English comedians complained
to a friend of mine that American audiences
laughed a great deal too soon for them, and took
the joke long before it was properly elucidated.
In the same way an American author, who had
formerly been connected with the *St. Nicholas*
magazine, was told by a London publisher that
the plan of it was all wrong. "These pages of
riddles at the end, for instance : no child would
ever guess them." And though the American
assured him that they were guessed regularly
every month in twenty thousand families, the
Englishmen still shook his head. Certainly the
difference between the national temperament
will be doubted by no American public speaker

in England who has had one of his hearers call
upon him the next morning to express satis-
faction in the clever anecdote which it had taken
his English auditor a night's meditation to comprehend.

It is impossible to overrate the value, in
developing an independent national feeling in
America, of the prolonged series of rather un-
amiable criticisms that have proceeded from the
English press and public men since the days of
Mrs. Trollope and down to our own day. It has
de-colonized us; and all the long agony of the
Civil War, when all the privileged classes in
England, after denouncing us through long
years for tolerating slavery, turned and de-
nounced us yet more bitterly for abolishing it
at the cost of our own heart's blood, only com-
pleted the emancipation. The way out of provincialism is to be frankly and even brutally
criticised; we thus learn not merely to see our
own faults, which is comparatively easy, but to
put our own measure on the very authority that
condemns us; *voir le monde, c'est juger les
juges.* We thus learn to trust our own temperament; to create our own methods; or, at

least, to select our own teachers. At this moment we go to France for our art and to Germany for our science as completely as if there were no such nation as England in the world. In literature the tie is far closer with what used to be called the mother country, and this because of the identity of language. All retrospective English literature — that is, all literature more than a century or two old — is common to the two countries. All contemporary literature cannot yet be judged, because it is contemporary. The time may come when not a line of current English poetry may remain except the four quatrains hung up in St. Margaret's Church, and when the Matthew Arnold of Macaulay's imaginary New Zealand may find with surprise that Whittier and Lowell produced something more worthy of that accidental immortality than Browning or Tennyson. The time may come when a careful study of even the despised American newspapers may reveal them to have been in one respect nearer to a high civilization than any of their European compeers; since the leading American literary journals criticise their own contributors with the utmost freedom, while there does not seem to be a journal in London or Paris that even attempts that courageous candor. To dwell merely on the faults and follies of a nascent nation is idle; vitality is always hopeful. To complain that a nation's very strength carries with it plenty of follies and excesses is, as Joubert says, to ask for a breeze that shall have the attribute of not blowing; *demander du vent qui n'ait point de mobilité.*

III

THE SHADOW OF EUROPE

WHEN the first ocean steamers crossed the Atlantic, about 1838, Willis predicted that they would only make American literature more provincial, by bringing Europe so much nearer than before. Yet Emerson showed that there was an influence at work more potent than steamers, and the colonial spirit in our literature began to diminish from his time. In the days of those first ocean voyages, the favorite literary journal of cultivated Americans was the New York *Albion*, which was conducted expressly for English residents on this continent; and it was considered a piece of American audacity when Horace Greeley called Margaret Fuller to New York, that the *Tribune* might give to our literature an organ of its own. Later, on the establishment of *Putnam's Magazine*, in 1853, I remember that one of the most enlightened New York journalists predicted to me the absolute failure of the whole enterprise. " Either an

American magazine will command no respect,"
he said, " or it must be better than *Blackwood*
or *Fraser*, which is an absurd supposition."
But either of our great illustrated magazines
has now more readers in England than *Fraser*
or *Blackwood* had then in America ; and to this
extent Willis's prediction is unfulfilled, and the
shadow of Europe is lifted, not deepened, over
our literature. But in many ways the glamour
of foreign superiority still holds ; and we still
see much of the old deferential attitude prevailing. Prince Albert said of Germany, in 1859,
that its rock ahead was self-sufficiency. In our
own country, as to literature and science, to say
nothing of art, our rock ahead is not self-sufficiency, but self-depreciation. Men still smile
at the Congressman who said, " What have we
to do with Europe ? " but I sometimes wish, for
the credit of the craft, that it had been a literary
man who said it. After all, it was only a
rougher paraphrase of Napoleon's equally trench-
ant words : " *Cette vieille Europe m'ennuie.*"

The young American who goes to London,
and finds there the most agreeable literary
society in the world, because the most central-

ized and compact, can hardly believe at first that the authors around him are made of the same clay with those whom he has often jostled on the sidewalk at home. He finds himself dividing his scanty hours between celebrated writers on the one side, and great historic remains on the other; as I can remember, one day, to have weighed a visit to Darwin against one to York Minster, and later to have postponed Stonehenge, which seemed likely to endure, for Tennyson, who perhaps might not. The young American sees in London, to quote Willis again, "whole shelves of his library walking about in coats and gowns," and they seem for the moment far more interesting than the similar shelves in home-made garments behind him. · He is not cured until he is some day startled with the discovery that there are cultivated foreigners to whom his own world is foreign, and therefore fascinating; men who think the better of him for having known Mark Twain, and women who are unwearied in their curiosity about the personal ways of Longfellow. Nay, when I once mentioned to that fine old Irish gentleman, the late Richard D. Webb, at his house in Dublin, that I had felt a thrill of pleasure on observing the street sign, denoting Fishamble Lane, at Cork, and recalling the ballad about "Misthress Judy McCarty, of Fishamble Lane," he pleased me by saying that he had felt just so in New York, when he saw the name of Madison Square, and thought of Miss Flora McFlimsey. So our modest continent had already its storied heroines and its hallowed ground!

There are, undoubtedly, points in which Europe, and especially England, has still the advantage of America; such, for instance, as weekly journalism. In regard to printed books there is also still an advantage in quantity, but not in quality; while in magazine literature the balance seems to incline just now the other way. I saw it claimed confidently, not long since, that the English magazines had " more solid value" than our own; but this solidity now consists, I should say, more in the style than in the matter, and is a doubtful benefit, like solidity in a pudding. When the writer whom I quote went on to cite the saying of a young girl, that she could always understand an

American periodical, but never opened an
English one without something unintelligible, it
seemed to me a bit of evidence whose bearing
was quite uncertain. It reminded me of a
delightful old lady, well known to me, who,
when taxed by her daughter with reading a book
quite beyond her comprehension, replied: "But
where is the use of reading a book that you can
understand? It does you no good." As a
matter of fact, the English magazines are
commonly not magazines at all, in the American
sense. Mr. M. D. Conway well said that the
Contemporary Review and the *Fortnightly* were
simply circular letters addressed by a few cultivated gentlemen to those belonging to the same
club. It is not until a man knows himself to
be writing for a hundred thousand readers that
he is compelled to work out his abstrusest
thought into clearness, just as a sufficient pres-
sure transforms opaque snow into pellucid ice.
In our great American magazines, history and
science have commonly undergone this process,
and the reader may be gratified, not ashamed,
at comprehending them.

The best remedy for too profound a deference

toward European literary work is to test the
author on some ground with which we in America cannot help being familiar. It is this which
makes a book of travels among us, or even a
lecturing trip, so perilous for a foreign reputation ; and among the few who can bear this test
— as De Tocqueville, Von Holst, the Comte de
Paris — it is singularly rare to find an Englishman. If the travellers have been thus unfortu-
nate, how much more those who have risked
themselves on cis-Atlantic themes without travelling. No living English writer stood higher
in America than Sir Henry Maine until we
watched him as he made the perilous transition
from " Ancient Law " to modern " Popular
Government," and saw him approaching what
he himself admits to be the most important theme
in modern history, with apparently but some half-
dozen authorities to draw upon, — the United
States Constitution, the *Federalist,* and two or
three short biographies. Had an American written on the most unimportant period of the most
insignificant German principality with a basis of
reading no larger, we should have wished that
his nationality had been kept a secret. It is

not strange, on such a method, tnat Maine
should inform us that the majority of the present State governments were formed before the
Union, and that only half the original thirteen
colonies held slaves. So Mr. John A. Doyle,
writing an extended history of American coloni-
zation, put into his first volume a map making
the lines of all the early grants run north and
south instead of east and west; and this having
been received with polite incredulity, gave us
another map depicting the New England colonies in 1700, with Plymouth still delineated as a
separate government, although it had been
united with Massachusetts eight years before.

When a lady in a London drawing-room
sends, by a returning New Yorker, an urgent
message to her cousin at Colorado Springs, we
rather enjoy it, and call it only pretty. Fanny's
way; she is not more ignorant of North American geography than we ourselves may be of that
of South America. But when we find that
English scholars of established reputation be-
tray, when on ground we know, defects of
method that seem hopeless, what reverence is
left for those who keep on ground that we do

not know?   In time, the shadow of Europe
must lose something of its impressiveness.   Dr.
Creighton, in his preface to the English "Historical Review," counts in all Americans as
merely so many "outlying English;" but it is
time to recognize that American literature is
not, and never again can be, merely an outlying
portion of the literature of England.

.

IV

ON TAKING OURSELVES SERIOUSLY

TOLSTOÏ says, in "Anna Karénina," that no nation will ever come to anything unless it attaches some importance to itself. (*Les seules nations qui aient de l'avenir, les seules qu'on puisse nommer historiques, sont celles qui sentent l'importance et le valeur de leur institutions.*) It is curious that ours seems to be the only contemporary nation which is denied this simple privilege of taking itself seriously. What is criticised in us is not so much that our social life is inadequate, as that we find it worth studying; not so much that our literature is insufficient, as that we think it, in Matthew Arnold's disdainful phrase, "important." In short, we are denied not merely the pleasure of being attractive to other people, which can easily be spared, but the privilege that is usually conceded to the humblest, of being of some interest to ourselves.

The bad results of this are very plain. They

are, indeed, so great that the evils which were supposed to come to our literature, for instance, from the absence of international copyright, seem trivial in comparison. The very persons who are working the hardest to elevate our civilization are constantly called from their duties, and, what is worse, are kept in a constant state of subdued exasperation, by the denial of their very right to do these duties. "My work," says Emerson, "may be of no importance, but I must not think it of no importance if I would do it well." Those of us who toiled for years to remove from this nation the stain of slavery, remember how, when the best blood of our kindred was lavished to complete the sacrifice, all the intellectual society of England turned upon us and reproached us for the deed. " The greatest war of principle which has been waged in this generation," wrote Motley in one of his letters, " was of no more interest to her, except as it bore upon the cotton question, than the wretched little squabbles of Mexico or South America."[1] And so those Americans who are spending their lives in the effort to remove the very defects visible in our

[1] Letters, I., 373.

letters, our arts, our literature, are met constantly by the insolent assumption, not that these drawbacks exist, but that they are not worth removing.

How magnificent, for instance, is the work constantly done among us, by private and public munificence, in the support of our libraries and schools. Carlyle, in one of his early journals, deplores that while every village around him has its place to lock up criminals, not one has a public library. In the State of Massachusetts this condition of things is coming to be reversed, since many villages have no jail, and free libraries will soon be universal. The writer is at this moment one of the trustees of three admirable donations just given by a young man not thirty-five to the city of his birth, — a city hall, a public library, and a manual training school. He is not a man of large fortune, as fortunes go, and his personal expenditures are on a very modest scale; he keeps neither yachts nor race-horses; his name never appears in the lists of fashionables, summer or winter; but he simply does his duty to American civilization in this way. There are multitudes of others, all over the land, who do the same sort of thing; they are the most essentially indigenous and American type we have, and their strength is in this, that they find their standard of action not abroad, but at home; they take their nation seriously. Yet this, which should be the thing that most appeals to every foreign observer, is, on the contrary, the very thing which the average foreign observer finds most offensive. " Do not tell me only," says Matthew Arnold, " . . . of the great and growing number of your churches and schools, libraries and newspapers; tell me also if your civilization — which is the grand name you give to all this development — tell me if your civilization is *interesting*."

Set aside the fact of transfer across an ocean; set aside the spectacle of a self-governing people; if there is no interest in the spectacle of a nation of sixty million people laboring with all its might to acquire the means and resources of civilized life, then there is nothing interesting on earth. A hundred years hence, the wonder will be, not that we Americans attached so much importance, at this stage, to these efforts of ours, but that even we appreciated their importance so little. If the calculations of Canon Zincke are correct, in his celebrated pamphlet, the civilization which we are organizing is the great civilization of the future. He computes that in 1980 the English-speaking population of the globe will be, at the present rate of progress, one billion ; and that of this number, eight hundred million will dwell in the United States. Now, all the interest we take in our schools, colleges, libraries, galleries, is but preliminary work in founding this great future civilization. Toils and sacrifices for this end may be compared, as Longfellow compares the secret studies of an author, to the submerged piers of a bridge : they are out of sight, but without them no structure can endure. If American society is really unimportant, and is foredoomed to fail, all these efforts will go with it; but if it has a chance of success, these are to be its foundations. If they are to be laid, they must be laid seriously. "No man can do anything well," says Emerson, "who does not think that what he does is the centre of the visible universe."

There is a prevailing theory, which seems to me largely flavored with cant, that we must accept with the utmost humility all foreign criticism, because it represents a remoter tribunal than our own. But the fact still remains, that while some things in art and literature are best judged from a distance, other things — including the whole department of local coloring — can be only judged near home. The better the work is done, in this aspect, the more essential it is that it should be viewed with knowledge. Looking at some marine sketches by a teacher of a good deal of note, the other day, I was led to point out the fact that she had given her schooner a jib, but had attached it to no bowsprit, and had anchored a whole fleet of dories by the stern instead of the bow. When I called the artist's attention to these peculiarities, the simple answer was: " I know nothing whatever about boats. I painted only what I saw, or thought I saw." In the same way one can scarcely open a foreign criticism on an American book, without seeing that, however good may be the abstract canons of criticism adopted, the detailed comment is as

confused as if a landsman were writing about
seamanship. When, for instance, a vivacious
Londoner like Mr. Andrew Lang attempts to
deal with that profound imaginative creation,
Arthur Dimmesdale, in the "Scarlet Letter,"
he fails to comprehend him from an obvious
and perhaps natural want of acquaintance with
the whole environment of the man. To Mr.
Lang he is simply a commonplace clerical Love-
lace, a dissenting clergyman caught in a shabby
intrigue. But if this clever writer had known
the Puritan clergy as we know them, the high-
priests of a Jewish theocracy, with the whole
work of God in a strange land resting on
their shoulders, he would have comprehended
the awful tragedy in this tortured soul, and
would have seen in him the profoundest and
most minutely studied of all Hawthorne's
characterizations. The imaginary offender for
whom that great author carried all winter, as
Mrs. Hawthorne told me, "a knot in his fore-
head," is not to be viewed as if his tale were a
mere chapter out of the "Mémoires de Casa-
nova."

When, at the beginning of this century,

Isaiah Thomas founded the American Antiquarian Society, he gave it as one of his avowed objects "that the library should contain a complete collection of the works of American authors." There was nothing extravagant, at that time, in the supposition that a single library of moderate size might do this; and the very impossibility of such an inclusion, at this day, is in part the result of the honest zeal with which Isaiah Thomas recognized the "importance" of our nascent literature. A disparaging opinion of any of these American books, or of all of them, does no more harm than the opinion of Pepys, that "Comus" was "an insipid, ridiculous play." In many cases the opinion will be well deserved; in few cases will it do any permanent harm. Since Emerson, we have ceased to be colonial, and have therefore ceased to be over-sensitive. The only danger is that, Emerson being dead, there should be a slight reaction toward colonial diffidence once more; that we should again pass through the apologetic period; that we should cease for a time to take ourselves seriously.

V

A COSMOPOLITAN STANDARD

IT has lately become the fashion in the United States to talk of the cosmopolitan standard as the one thing needful; to say that formerly American authors were judged by their own local tribunals, but henceforth they must be appraised by the world's estimate. The trouble is, that for most of those who reason in this way, cosmopolitanism does not really mean the world's estimate, but only the judgment of Europe — a judgment in which America itself is to have no voice. Like the trade-winds which so terrified the sailors of Columbus, it blows only from the eastward. There is no manner of objection to cosmopolitanism, if the word be taken in earnest. There is something fine in the thought of a federal republic of letters, a vast literary tribunal of nations, in which each nation has a seat; but this is just the kind of cosmopolitanism which these critics do not seek. They seek merely a far-off judgment, and this is no better than a local tribunal; in some respects it is worse. The remotest standard of judgment that I ever encountered was that of the late Professor Ko-Kun-Hua, of Harvard University. There was something delicious in looking into his serene and inscrutable face, and in trying to guess at the operations of a highly trained mind, to which the laurels of Plato and Shakespeare were as absolutely unimportant as those of the Sweet Singer of Michigan; yet the tribunal which he afforded could hardly be called cosmopolitan. He undoubtedly stood, however, for the oldest civilization; and it seemed trivial to turn from his serene Chinese indifference, and attend to children of a day like the *Revue des deux Mondes* and the *Saturday Review*. If we are to recognize a remote tribunal, let us by all means prefer one that has some maturity about it.

But it is worth while to remember that, as a matter of fact, the men who created the American government gave themselves very little concern about cosmopolitanism, but simply went about their own work. They took hints from older nations, and especially from the mother country, but they acknowledged no jurisdiction there. The consensus of the civilized world, then and for nearly a century after, viewed the American government as a mere experiment, and republican institutions as a bit of short-lived folly; yet the existence of the new nation gave it a voice henceforth in every tribunal calling itself cosmopolitan. Henceforth that word includes the judgment of the New World on the Old, as well as that of the Old World on the New; and when we construe literary cosmopolitanism in the same way, we shall be on as firm ground in literature as in government.

So long as we look merely outside of ourselves for a standard, we are as weak as if we looked merely inside of ourselves; probably weaker, for timidity is weaker than even the arrogance of strength. There is no danger that the foreign judgment will not duly assert itself; the danger is, that our own self-estimate will be too apologetic. What with courtesy and good-nature, and a lingering of the old colonialism, we are not yet beyond the cringing period in our literary judgment. The obeisance of all good society in London before a successful cir-

cus-manager from America was only a shade
more humiliating than the reverential attention
visible in the American press when Matthew
Arnold was kind enough to stand on tiptoe upon
our lecture-platform and apply his little meas-
uring-tape to the great shade of Emerson. I
should like to see in our literature some of the
honest self-assertion shown by Senator Tracy of
Litchfield, Connecticut, during Washington's
administration, in his reply to the British Min-
ister's praises of Mrs. Oliver Wolcott's beauty.
" Your countrywoman," said the Englishman,
" would be admired at the Court of St. James."
— " Sir," said Tracy, " she is admired even on
Litchfield Hill."

In that recent book of aphorisms which has
given a fresh impulse to the fading fame of Dr.
Channing, he points out that the hope of the
world lies in the fact that parents can *not* make
of their children what they will. It is equally
true of parent nations. How easily we accept
the little illusions offered us by our elders in
the world's literature, almost forgetting that
two and two make four, in the innocent delight
with which they inspire us ! In re-reading Scott's

"Old Mortality" the other day, I was pleased
to find myself still carried away by the author's
own grandiloquence, where he describes the
approach of Claverhouse and his men to the
castle of Tillietudlem. "The train was long and
imposing, for there were about two hundred
and fifty horse upon the march." Two hundred
and fifty! Yet I read it for the moment with
as little demur at these trivial statistics as if
our own Sheridan had never ridden out of Win-
chester at the head of ten thousand cavalry.
It is the same with all literature: we are asked
to take Europe at Europe's own valuation, and
then to take America at Europe's valuation also ;
and whenever we speak of putting an American
valuation upon the four quarters of the globe,
we are told that this will not do; this is not
cosmopolitan.

We are too easily misled, in exhorting American authors to a proper humility, because we
forget that the invention of printing has in a
manner placed all nations on a level. Literature is the only art whose choicest works are
easily transportable. Once secure a public library in every town — a condition now in pro-

cess of fulfilment in our older American States
— and every bright boy or girl has a literary
Louvre and Vatican at command.   Given a
taste for literature, and there are at hand all the
masters of the art — Plato and Homer, Cicero
and Horace, Dante, Shakespeare, and Goethe.
Travel is still needed, but not for books — only
for other forms of art, for variety of acquaint-
anceship, and for the habit of dealing with men
and women of many nationalities.   The most
fastidious American in Europe should not look
with shame, but with pride and hope, upon those
throngs of his fellow-countrymen whom he sees
crowding the art-galleries of Europe, looking
about them as ignorantly, if you please, as the
German barbarians when they entered Rome.
It is not so hard to gain culture; the thing
almost impossible to obtain, unless it be born in
us, is the spirit of initiative, of self-confidence.
That is the gift with which great nations begin;
we now owe our chief knowledge of Roman
literature and art to the descendants of those
Northern barbarians.

And it must be kept in view, finally, that a
cosmopolitan tribunal is at best but a court of

appeal, and is commonly valuable in proportion as the courts cf preliminary jurisdiction have done their duty. The best preparation for going abroad is to know the worth of what one has seen at home. I remember to have been impressed with a little sense of dismay, on first nearing the shores of Europe, at the thought of what London and Paris might show me in the way of great human personalities; but I said to myself, "To one who has heard Emerson lecture, and Parker preach, and Garrison thunder, and Phillips persuade, there is no reason why Darwin or Victor Hugo should pass for more than mortal;" and accordingly they did not. We shall not prepare ourselves for a cosmopolitan standard by ignoring our own great names or undervaluing the literary tradition that has produced them. When Stuart Newton, the artist, was asked, on first arriving in London from America, whether he did not enjoy the change, he answered honestly, " I here see such society occasionally, as I saw at home all the time." At this day the self-respecting American sometimes hears admissions in Europe which make him feel that we are already creating a standard, not waiting to be judged by one. The most variously accomplished literary critic in England, the late Mark Pattison, said to me of certain American books then lately published, " Is such careful writing appreciated in the United States? It would not be in England." On the shores of a new continent, then, there was already a standard which was in one respect better than the cosmopolitan.

VI

A CONTEMPORANEOUS POSTERITY

THERE is an American novel, now pretty effectually forgotten, which yet had the rare honor of contributing one permanent phrase to English literature. I remember well the surprise produced, in my boyhood, by the appearance of "Stanley; or, The Recollections of a Man of the World." It was so crammed with miscellaneous literary allusion and criticism, after the fashion of those days, that it was attributed by some critics to Edward Everett, then the standing representative of omniscience in our Eastern States. This literary material was strung loosely upon a plot wild and improbable enough for Brockden Brown, and yet vivid enough to retain a certain charm, for me at least, even until this day. It was this plot, perhaps, which led the late James T. Fields to maintain that Maturin was the author of the novel in question; but it is now known to have been the production of Horace Binney Wallace

of Philadelphia, then a youth of twenty-one.
In this book occurs the sentence: "Byron's
European fame is the best earnest of his immortality, for a foreign nation is a kind of contemporaneous posterity." [1]

Few widely quoted phrases have had, I fancy,
less foundation. It is convenient to imagine
that an ocean or a mountain barrier, or even a
line of custom houses, may furnish a sieve that
shall sift all true reputations from the chaff;
but in fact, I suspect, whatever whims may vary
or unsettle immediate reputations on the spot,
these disturbing influences are only redistrib-
uted, not abolished, by distance. Whether we
look to popular preference or to the judgment
of high authorities, the result is equally baf-
fling. Napoleon Bonaparte preferred Ossian, it
is said, to Shakespeare; and Voltaire placed the
latter among the minor poets, viewing him at
best as we now view Marlowe, as the author of
an occasional mighty line. It was after Mrs.
Elizabeth Montagu had been asked to hear Voltaire demolish Shakespeare at an evening party
in Paris that she made her celebrated answer,

[1] ii. 89.

when the host expressed the hope that she had not been pained by the criticism : " Why should I be pained? I have not the honor to be among the intimate friends of M. de Voltaire." Even at this day the French journalists are quite bewildered by the *Pall Mall Gazette's* lists of English immortals ; and ask who Tennyson is, and what plays Ruskin has written. Those who happened, like myself, to be in Paris during the Exposition of 1878 remember well the astonishment produced in the French mind by the discovery that any pictures were painted in England ; and the French Millet was at that time almost as little known in London as was his almost namesake, the English Millais, in Paris. If a foreign nation represented posterity, neither of these eminent artists appeared then to have a chance of lasting fame.

When we see the intellectual separation thus maintained between England and France, with only the width of the Channel between them, we can understand the separation achieved by the Atlantic, even where there is no essential difference of language. M. Taine tries to convince Frenchmen that the forty English " immortals" selected by the readers of the *Pall Mall Gazette* are equal, taken together, to the French Academicians. "You do not know them, you say?" he goes on. "That is not a sufficient reason. The English, and all who speak English, know them well, but, on the other hand, know little of our men of letters." After this a French paper, reprinting a similar English list, added comments on the names, like this: "Robert Browning, the Scotch poet." There is probably no better manual of universal knowledge than the great French dictionary of Larousse. When people come with miscellaneous questions to the Harvard College librarians, they often say in return, "Have you looked in Larousse?" Now, when one looks in Larousse to see who Robert Browning was, one finds the statement that the genius of Browning is more analogous to that of his American contemporaries "Emerton, Wendell Holmes, and Bigelow" than to that of any English poet (*celle de n'importe quel poëte anglais.*) This transformation of Emerson into Emerton, and of Lowell, probably, to Bigelow, is hardly more extraordinary than to link together three such dissimilar poets, and compare Browning to all three of them, or, indeed, to either of the three. Yet it gives us the high-water mark of what "contemporaneous posterity" has to offer. The criticism of another nation can, no doubt, offer some advantages of its own — a fresh pair of eyes and freedom from cliques; but a foreigner can be no judge of local coloring, whether in nature or manners. The mere knowledge of the history of a nation may be essential to a knowledge of its art.

So far as literature goes, the largest element of foreign popularity lies naturally in some kinship of language. Reputation follows the line of least resistance. The Germanic races take naturally to the literature of their own congeners, and so with the Latin. As these last have had precedence in organizing the social life of the world, so they still retain it in their literary sway. The French tongue, in particular, while ceasing to be the vehicle of all travelling intercourse, is still the second language of all the world. A Portuguese gentleman said once to a friend of mine that he was studying French "in order to have something to read." All the empire of Great Britain, circling the globe, affords to her poets or novelists but a petty and insular audience compared with that addressed by George Sand or Victor Hugo. A Roman Catholic convert from America, going from Paris to Rome, and having audience with a former pope, is said to have been a little dismayed when his Holiness instantly inquired, with eager solicitude, as to the rumored illness of Paul de Kock — the milder Zola of the last generation. In contemporaneous fame, then, the mere accident of nationality and language plays an enormous part; but this accident will clearly have nothing to do with the judgment of posterity.

If any foreign country could stand for a contemporaneous posterity, one would think it might be a younger nation judging an older one. Yet how little did the American reputations of fifty years ago afford any sure prediction of permanent fame in respect to English writers! True, we gave early recognition to Carlyle and Tennyson, but scarcely greater than to authors now faded or fading into obscurity, — Milnes (Lord Houghton), Sterling,

Trench, Alford, and Bailey. No English poem, it was said, ever sold through so many American editions as "Festus;" nor was Tupper's "Proverbial Philosophy" far behind it. Translators and publishers quarrelled bitterly for the privilege of translating Frederika Bremer's novels; but our young people, who already stand for posterity, hardly recall her name. I asked a Swedish commissioner at our Centennial Exhibition in 1876, "Is Miss Bremer still read in Sweden?" He shook his head; and when I asked, "Who has replaced her?" he said, "Bret Harte and Mark Twain." It seemed the irony of fame; and there is no guaranty that this reversed national compliment will, any more than our recognition of her, predict the judgment of the future.

If this uncertainty exists when the New World judges the Old, of which it knows something, the insecurity must be greater when the Old World judges the New, of which it knows next to nothing. If the multiplicity of translations be any test, Mrs. Stowe's contemporary fame, the world over, has been unequalled in literature; but will any one now say that it

surely predicts the judgment of posterity?
Consider the companion instances.   Next to
" Uncle Tom's Cabin " ranked for a season,
doubtless, in European favor, that exceedingly
commonplace novel " The Lamplighter," whose
very name is now almost forgotten at home.   It
is impossible to say what law enters into such
successes as this last; but one of the most
obvious demands made by all foreign contemporary judgment is, that an American book
should supply to a jaded public the element of
the unexpected.   Europe demands from America not so much a new thought and purpose, as
some new *dramatis personæ ;* that an author
should exhibit a wholly untried type, — an
Indian, as Cooper; a negro, as Mrs. Stowe; a
mountaineer, as Miss Murfree ; a California
gambler, as Bret Harte ; a rough or roustabout,
as Whitman.

There are commonly two ways to eminent
social success for an American in foreign
society, — to be more European than Europeans
themselves, or else to surpass all other Americans in some amusing peculiarity which foreigners suppose to be American.   It is much

the same in literature. Lady Morgan, describing the high society of Dublin in her day, speaks of one man as a great favorite who always entered every drawing-room by turning a somersault. This is one way of success for an American book; but the other way, which is at least more dignified, is rarely successful except when combined with personal residence and private acquaintance. Down to the year 1880 Lowell was known in England, almost exclusively, as the author of the "Biglow Papers," and was habitually classed with Artemus Ward and Josh Billings, except that his audience was smaller. The unusual experience of a diplomatic appointment first unveiled to the English mind the all-accomplished Lowell whom we mourn. In other cases, as with Prescott and Motley, there was the mingled attraction of European manners and a European subject. But a simple and home-loving American, who writes upon the themes furnished by his own nation, without pyrotechnics or fantastic spelling, is apt to seem to the English mind quite uninteresting. There is nothing which ordinarily interests Europeans less than an

Americanism unaccompanied by a war-whoop. The *Saturday Review*, wishing to emphasize its contempt for Henry Ward Beecher, finally declares that one would turn from him with relief even to the poems of Whittier.

There could hardly have been a more exhaustive proof of this local limitation or *chauvinisme* than I myself noticed at a London dinner-party some years ago. Our host was an Oxford professor, and the company was an eminent one. Being hard pressed about American literature, I had said incidentally that a great deal of intellectual activity in America was occupied, and rightly, by the elucidation of our own history, — a thing, I added, which inspired almost no interest in England. This fact being disputed, I said, "Let us take a test case. We have in America an historian superior to Motley in labors, in originality of treatment, and in style. If he had, like Motley, first gone abroad for a subject, and then for a residence, his European fame would have equalled Motley's. As it is, probably not a person present except our host will recognize his name." When I mentioned Francis Parkman, the prediction was fulfilled. All, save the host — a man better acquainted with the United States, perhaps, than any living Englishman — confessed utter ignorance: an ignorance shared, it seems, by the only English historian of American literature, Professor Nichol, who actually does not allude to Parkman. It seems to me that we had better, in view of such facts, dismiss the theory that a foreign nation is a kind of contemporaneous posterity.

VII

ON LITERARY TONICS

SOME minor English critic wrote lately of
Dr. Holmes's "Life of Emerson:" "The
Boston of his day does not seem to have been a
very strong place; we lack performance." This
is doubtless to be attributed rather to ignorance
than to that want of seriousness which Mr.
Stedman so justly points out among the younger
Englishmen. The Boston of which he speaks
was the Boston of Garrison and Phillips, of
Whittier and Theodore Parker; it was the
headquarters of those old-time abolitionists of
whom the English Earl of Carlisle wrote that
they were "fighting a battle without a parallel
in the history of ancient or modern heroism."
It was also the place which nurtured those young
Harvard students who are chronicled in the
"Harvard Memorial Biographies" — those who
fell in the war of the Rebellion; those of whom
Lord Houghton once wrote tersely to me:
"They are men whom Europe has learned to

honor and would do well to imitate." The service of all these men, and its results, give a measure of the tonic afforded in the Boston of that day. Nay, Emerson himself was directly responsible for much of their strength. "To him more than to all other causes together," says Lowell, "did the young martyrs of our Civil War owe the sustaining strength of moral heroism that is so touching in every record of their lives." And when the force thus developed in Boston and elsewhere came to do its perfect work, that work turned out to be the fighting of a gigantic war and the freeing of four millions of slaves; and this in the teeth of every sympathy and desire of all that appeared influential in England. This is what is meant, in American history at least, by "performance."

Indeed, as the War of 1812 has been called, following a suggestion of Franklin's, "the second War for Independence," so the Civil War might be called in the same sense the third war of the same kind; and the evolution of the American as a type wholly new and distinct from the Englishman, dates largely from that event. We are sometimes misled by a few

imitations in respect to visiting cards and ser-
vants' liveries, to be solicitous about a revival
of Anglomania, forgetting that the very word
Anglomania implies separation and weaning.   I
can recall when there was no more room for
Anglomania in New York than in Piccadilly,
for the simple reason that all was still English;
when the one cultivated newspaper in the country was the New York *Albion*, conducted for
British residents ; when the scene of every child's
story was laid abroad and not at home; when
Irving was read in America because he wrote
of England, and Cooper's novels were regarded
as a sort of daring eccentricity of the frontier.
Fifty years ago Anglomania could scarcely be
said to exist in this country; for the nation was
still, for all purposes of art and literature, a mere
province of England.   Now all is changed ; the
literary tone of the United States is more serious,
more original, and, in its regard for external
forms, more cultivated than that now prevailing
on the other side.   Untravelled Americans still
feel a sense of awe before the English press,
which vanishes when they visit London and talk
with the young fellows who write for its jour-

nals; and when these youths visit us, what light-
weights they are apt to seem!

Emerson said of our former literary allegiance
to England that it was the tax we paid for the
priceless gift of English literature; but this tax
should surely not be now a heavy one; a few
ballades and *villanelles* seem the chief recent
importations. The current American criticism
on the latest English literature is that it is
brutal or trivial. The London correspondent of
the *Critic* quoted some Englishmen the other
day as saying that the principal results of our
Civil War had been "the development of Henry
James, and the adoption of Mr. Robert Stevenson." Mr. Stevenson, if adopted, can hardly
be brought into the discussion. Mr. James has
no doubt placed himself as far as possible
beyond reach of the Civil War by keeping the
Atlantic Ocean between him and the scene
where it occurred; but when I recall that I
myself saw his youngest brother, still almost a
boy, lying near to death, as it then seemed, in
a hospital at Beaufort, S. C., after the charge on
Fort Wagner, I can easily imagine that the
Civil War may really have done something

for Mr. James's development, after all. Mr.
Howells has scarcely yet given up taking the
heroes of his books from among those who had
gone through a similar ordeal, and it will be
many years before the force of that great impulse is spent. For one thing, the results of the
war have liberated the Southern literary genius,
and that part of the nation, so strangely unpro-
lific till within twenty-five years, is now arrest-
ing its full share of attention, and perhaps even
more than its share.

It is difficult to say just how far the influence
of a literary tonic extends, and Goethe might
doubtless be cited as an instance where art
was its own sufficient stimulus. In the cases of
a writer like Poe, we trace no tonic element.
The great anti-slavery agitation and the general
reformatory mood of half a century ago undoubtedly gave us Channing, Emerson, Whittier, Longfellow, and Lowell; not that they
would not have been conspicuous in any case,
but that the moral attribute in their natures
might have been far less marked. The great
temporary fame of Mrs. Stowe was identified
with the same influence. Hawthorne and

Holmes were utterly untouched by the anti-
slavery agitation, yet both yielded to the excitement of the war, and felt in some degree its
glow. It elicited from Aldrich his noble Fredericksburg sonnet. Stedman, Stoddard, and
Bayard Taylor wrote war songs, as did Julia
Ward Howe conspicuously. Whitman's poem
on the death of Lincoln is, in my judgment, one
of the few among his compositions which will
live. Wallace, who must be regarded as on
the whole our most popular novelist — whatever
may be thought of the quality of his work —
won his first distinction in the Civil War. Cable,
Lanier, Thompson, and other strong writers
were also engaged in it, on the Confederate side.
It is absolutely impossible to disentangle from
the work of any but the very youngest of our
living American authors that fibre of iron which
came from our great Civil War and the stormy
agitation that led up to it.

What is to succeed that great tonic? — for
we can hardly suppose that the human race is
to be kept forever at war for the sake of sup-
plying a series of heroic crises. It is evident
that no particular source of moral stimulus is

essential; the Woman Suffrage movement has made a dozen and more women into orators and authors; and Helen Jackson was as thoroughly thrilled and inspired by the wrongs of the American Indians, as was Mrs. Stowe by those of the Negroes. The American writers who signed the petition for the pardon of the Chicago Anarchists, had at least the wholesome experience of standing firmly, whether they were right or wrong, against the current opinion of those around them. The contributions toward the discussion of social questions which have of late flowed so freely from clergymen and other non-experts, must undoubtedly do good to those from whom they proceed, if to no others. The essential thing is that the literary man should be interested in something which he feels to be of incomparably more importance to the universe than the development of his own pretty talent. We see the same thing across the ocean, when Swinburne writes his "Song in Time of Order," and Morris marches in a Socialist procession. Here lies the power of the Russian writers, of Victor Hugo. Probably no man who ever lived had an egotism more colossal than

that of Hugo, yet he was large enough to subordinate even that egotism to the aims that
absorbed him — to abhorrence of Napoleon the
Little — to enthusiasm for the golden age of
man. I like to think of him as I saw him at the
Voltaire Centenary in 1876, pleading for Universal Peace amid the alternate hush and roar
of thousands of excitable Parisians — his lion-
like head erect, his strong hand uplifted, his
voice still powerful at nearly eighty years. So
vast was the crowd, so deserted the neighbor-
ing streets, that it all recalled the words put by
Landor into the lips of Demosthenes : " I have
seen the day when the most august of cities
had but one voice within her walls ; and when
the stranger on entering them stopped at the
silence of the gateway, and said, ' Demosthenes
is speaking in the assembly of the people.' "

VIII

THE FEAR OF THE DEAD LEVEL

IT is noticeable ι foreign observers, who were always a little ̃ious about the possible monotony of our society, have grown a little more so since they have ventured west of the Alleghanies and crossed the long plain to be traversed before reaching the Rocky Mountains. In the days when an American trip culminated at Niagara, and even Trenton Falls was considered a sight so remarkable that Charles Sumner wrote from England to caution a traveller by no means to quit the country without seeing it, there was no complaint that our scenery was monotonous. The continent was supposed to have done all, in that line, which could fairly be asked of it. Since then, the criticism has grown with the railway journey, and people fear that the horizontal line of the prairies must more than counterbalance the vertical line of Niagara, in moulding the American mind. Then these very travellers are justly anxious about the sameness of our cities; the streets numbered one way, the avenues the other. "Can the young heart," they ask, "attach definite associations or tender emotions with an Arabic figure? Is there romance in numeration?" Probably they carry the criticism too far. As Nature, according to Emerson, loves the number five, so does the well-bred New Yorker. Surely "Fifth Avenue" has as definite and distinctive a meaning for him as if there were no other number in the universe; and I am sure that in every city there is some youth who cannot look up at the street-sign denoting some Twenty-third Street or Thirty-fifth Street without a slight spasm of the heart. Such associations last a great while, even if the street be disagreeable; the philosopher Descartes was enamored in his youth with a young lady who squinted a little, and it is said that he never through life could behold without the tenderest emotion a woman having a cast in her eye. If Descartes was permanently sentimental about orbs that were crooked, cannot others be so about streets that are straight?

Still, in the long run, monotony is not satis-

fying; and the kind traveller hastens to con-
ciliate local pride by granting some individuality
to a few cities, such as New York, Washington,
Chicago, New Orleans, Boston. It is very
possible that a closer student of this particular
point might find less monotony, even among
towns, than he does. In Mr. Warner's late
studies of American cities, for instance, we are
struck, not with the sameness, but with the
variety. Much depends upon the trained eye.
A long railway trip across a level plain is
monotonous to one who is looking for bold
scenery; but it may not be monotonous to the
agriculturist who is studying the crops, or to
the botanist who is looking out for trees and
wild flowers, or to the student of human nature
who is watching for new types of character. So
an exhibition of machinery is monotonous to the
ignorant, but full of knowledge to the expert;
and there was a capital illustration in *Punch* at
the time of the first International Exposition in
London, showing the difference between a
group of bored fashionables, passing languidly
through the hall devoted to new inventions, and
a party of intelligent mechanics eagerly exam-

ining a machine. So of human beings: to a raw officer of colored troops, for instance, in the Civil War, his men looked hopelessly alike as they stood uniformed in line; but he soon found that every face had its individuality. I have even heard teachers say the same of a new class, black or white, on its entering school. Living in a college town, I find the young men looking so much the same, so long as I do not know them, as to suggest the wish expressed by Humpty Dumpty to Alice, that some human beings could be constructed with their features differently combined — the noses, for instance, being sometimes put above the eyebrows — in order to distinguish them more conspicuously. Yet each one becomes on acquaintance a perfectly defined personality; and it is complained by their professors that there is sometimes rather an excess of individuality, when it comes to discipline.

It turns out, then, that individuality depends largely on the observer. Thoreau points out that no two oak-leaves are precisely alike; and Scudder says the same of the markings on butterflies' wings. Alexander von Humboldt

remarked that this trait develops with civilization; a hundred wild dogs are more alike
than their domesticated kindred, and so of a
hundred wild men. If the step we have taken
in America, away from courts and hereditary
institutions, be a step in civilization, then it is
certainly to lead to more individuality, not less.
Even in England, where is marked individuality
to be found? Surely, among the men who have
made the name of England great; her artists,
authors, inventors, scientific teachers. Yet Mr.
Besant has lately pointed out, in a very impressive passage, that scarcely one of these men
ever went near the court of England. The
marked individuality of that nation, therefore,
is distinctly outside of the court circle; and, if
so, individuality would gain and not lose by
dropping those circles altogether. The difficulty is that the court circle substitutes for
this quality a mere variation of costume — a
robe, a decoration. But in reality these things
subdue individuality, instead of developing it;
as every recruiting officer found, during our
Civil War, that recruits became more docile the
moment they put on the uniform; and a lady

at Newport once vindicated to me the desirable-
ness of liveries on the ground that they were
" very repressive." In persons of higher grade
in England there is developed the official — the
Lord Chamberlain, the Lord of the Hounds ; or
the typical hereditary lord, in perhaps two different types, " the wicked lord," and " the good
lord ; " but there is no added development of
the individual.

It all comes to this, then, that for the development of individuality you must have a free
career; and the guarantee of freedom is the
first step toward what you seek. Nowhere will
you find a more racy personality than among
New England farmers, whose fathers lived
before them on the same soil, or perhaps six
generations of ancestors, and who, among all
restrictions of hard soil and severe competition,
have yet kept their separate characteristics. I
have spent summer after summer in the country,
and have never yet encountered two farmers
alike — two who would not, even if drawn by
an unsympathetic though acute observer like
Howells, stand out on the canvas with as
marked an individuality as Silas Lapham. It

is so with our native-born population generally. In the best volume of New England stories ever written — it is perhaps needless to say that I refer to "Five Hundred Dollars a Year and Other Stories," by Mr. H. W. Chaplin — there is an inimitable scene in a jury-room where the hero, "Eli," holds out during many hours for the innocence of a wronged man. The jurymen are commonplace personages enough — a sea captain, a butcher, a pedler, and so on — and yet their talk through page after page brings out in each a type of character so vivid and distinct that you feel sure that you would know each interlocutor afterward, if you met him in the street. He who approaches human nature in such a spirit need have no fear of the dead level.

IX

DO WE NEED A LITERARY CENTRE?

IN the latter days of the last French Empire some stir was made by a book claiming that Paris was already the capital of the world — *Paris capitale du monde*. Mr. Lowell has lately made claims rather more moderate for London, suggesting that a time may come when the English-speaking race will practically control the planet, having London for its centre, with all roads leading to it, as they once led to Rome. But it is plain that in making this estimate Mr. Lowell overlooked some very essential factors — for instance, himself. If ancient Rome had borrowed for its most important literary addresses an orator from Paphlagonia, who was not even a Roman citizen, it would plainly have ceased to be the Rome of our reverence; and yet this is what has repeatedly been done in London by the selection of Mr. Lowell. Or if the province of Britain had furnished a periodical publication — an *Acta*

Eruditorum, let us say — which had been regularly reprinted in Rome with a wider circulation than any metropolitan issue, then Rome
would again have ceased to be Rome; and yet
this is what is done in London every month by
the American illustrated magazines. It is
clear, then, that London is not the exclusive
intellectual centre of the English-speaking
world, nor is there the slightest evidence that
it is becoming more and more such a centre.
On the contrary, one hears in England a prolonged groan over an imagined influence the
other way. "I have long felt," wrote Sir
Frederick Elliot to Sir Henry Taylor from
London (December 20, 1877), "that the most
certain of political tendencies in England is
what, for want of a better name, I will call the
Yankeeizing tendency." But apart from these
suggestions as to London, Mr. Lowell has
urged and urged strongly the need of a national capital. He has expressed the wish for
"a focus of intellectual, moral, and material
activity," "a common head, as well as a common body." In this he errs only, as it seems to
me, in applying too readily to our vaster con-

ditions the standards and traditions of much smaller countries. If it be true, as was said the other day by our eloquent English-born clergyman in New York, Dr. Rainsford, that America is a branch which is rapidly becoming the main stem, then the fact may as well be recognized. As in our political system, so in literature, we may need a new plan of structure for that which is to embrace a continent — a system of co-ordinate states instead of a centralized empire. Our literature, like our laws, will probably proceed not from one focus, but from many. To one looking across from London or Paris this would seem impossible, for while living in a great city you come to feel as if that spot were all the world, and all else must be abandoned, as Cherbuliez's heroine says, to the indiscreet curiosity of geographers. But when you again look at that city from across the ocean, you perceive how easily it may cramp and confine those who live in it, and you are grateful for elbow-room and fresh air. Nothing smaller than a continent can really be large enough to give space for the literature of the future.

It is to be considered that in this age great

cities do not exhibit, beyond a certain point, the breadth of atmosphere that one expects from a world's capital. On the contrary, we find in Paris, in Berlin, in London, a certain curious narrowness, an immense exaggeration of its own petty and local interests. We meet there individual men of extraordinary knowledge in this or that direction, but the interchange of thought and feeling seems to lie within a ring-fence. A good test of this is in the recent books of " reminiscences " or " remembrances " by accomplished men who have lived for years in the most brilliant circles of London. Each day is depicted as a string of pearls, but with only the names of the pearls mentioned; the actual jewels are not forthcoming. A man breakfasts with one circle of wits and sages, lunches with another, dines with a third; and all this intellectual affluence yields him for his diary perhaps a single anecdote or repartee no better than are to be found by dozens in the corners of American country newspapers. It recalls what a clever American artist once told me, that he had dined triumphantly through three English counties, and brought away a great social reputation, on the strength of the stories in one old "Farmer's Almanac" which he had put in his trunk to protect some books on leaving home. The very excess or congestion of intellect in a great city seems to defeat itself; there is no time or strength left for anything beyond the most superficial touch-and-go intercourse; it is *persiflage* carried to the greatest perfection, but you get little more.

A great metropolis is moreover disappointing, because, although it may furnish great men, its literary daily bread is inevitably supplied by small men, who revolve round the larger ones, and who are even less interesting to the visitor than the same class at home. There is something amusing in the indifference of every special neighborhood to all literary gossip except its own. For instance, one might well have supposed that the admiration of Englishmen for Longfellow might inspire an intelligent desire to know something of his daily interests, of his friendships and pursuits; yet when his Memoirs appeared, all English critics pronounced these things exceedingly uninteresting; while much

smaller gossip about much smaller people, in
the Hayward Memoirs, was found by these same
critics to be an important addition to the history
of the times. It is an absolute necessity for
every nation, as for every age, to insist on setting its own standard, even to the resolute re-
adjustment of well-established reputations. So
long as it does not, it will find itself overawed
and depressed, not as much by the greatness of
some metropolis, as by its littleness.

It is the calamity of a large city that its
smallest men appear to themselves important
simply because they dwell there; just as Trav-
ers, the New York wit, explained his stutter-
ing more in that city than in Baltimore, on
the ground that it was a larger place. The
London literary journals seem to an American
visitor to be largely filled with *Epistolæ obscuro-
rum virorum ;* and when I attended, some years
since, the first meetings of the *Association
Littéraire Internationale* in Paris, it was impossible not to be impressed by the multitude of
minor literary personages, among whom a writer
so·mediocre as Edmond About towered as a
giant. But no doubts of their own supreme

importance to the universe appeared to beset
these young gentlemen: —

> " How many thousand never heard the name
>   Of Sidney or of Spenser, or their books ?
> And yet brave fellows, and presume of fame,
>   And think to bear down all the world with looks."

One was irresistibly reminded, in their society,
of these lines of old Daniel; or of the comfort-
able self-classification of another Frenchman,
M. Vestris, the dancer, who always maintained
that there were but three really great men in
Europe — Voltaire, Frederick II., and himself.
We talk about small places as being Little Pedlingtons, but it sometimes seems as if the Great
Pedlingtons were the smallest, after all, because
there is nobody to teach them humility. Little
Pedlington at least shows itself apologetic and
even uneasy; that is what saves it to reason and
common-sense. But fancy a Parisian apologiz-
ing for Paris !

The great fear of those who demand an intellectual metropolis is provincialism; but we
must remember that the word is used in two
wholly different senses, which have nothing in
common. What an American understands by

provincialism is best to be seen in the little
French town, some imaginary Tarascon or Car-
cassonne, where the notary and the physician
and the *rentiers* sit and play dominoes and
feebly disport themselves in a benumbed world
of petty gossip. But what the Parisian or the
Londoner would assume to be provincial among
us is an American town, perhaps of the same size,
but which has already its schools and its public
library well established, and is now aiming at
a gallery of art and a conservatory of music.
To confound these opposite extremes of development under one name is like confounding
childhood and second childhood; the one representing all promise, the other all despair. Mr.
Henry James, who proves his innate kindness
of heart by the constancy with which he is always pitying somebody, turns the full fervor of
his condolence on Hawthorne for dwelling amid
the narrowing influences of a Concord atmosphere. But if those influences gave us "The
Scarlet Letter" and Emerson's "Essays," does
it not seem almost a pity that we cannot extend
that same local atmosphere, as President Lincoln proposed to do with Grant's whiskey, to
some of our other generals?

The dweller in a metropolis has the advantage, if such it be, of writing immediately for a few thousand people, all whose prejudices he knows and perhaps shares. He writes to a picked audience; but he who dwells in a country without a metropolis has the immeasurably greater advantage of writing for an audience which is, so to speak, unpicked, and which, therefore, includes the picked one, as an apple includes its core. One does not need to be a very great author in America to find that his voice is heard across a continent — a thing more stimulating and more impressive to the imagination than the morning drum-beat of Great Britain. The whole vast nation, but a short time since, was simultaneously following the "Rise of Silas Lapham," or "The Casting Away of Mrs. Lecks and Mrs. Aleshine." In a few years the humblest of the next generation of writers will be appealing to a possible constituency of a hundred millions. He who writes for a metropolis may unconsciously share its pettiness; he who writes for a hundred millions must feel some expansion in his thoughts, even though his and theirs be still crude. Keats asked his friend to throw a copy of "Endymion" into the heart of the African desert; is it not better to cast your book into a vaster region that is alive with men?

Cliques lose their seeming importance where one has the human heart at his door. That calamity which Fontenelle mourned, the loss of so many good things by their being spoken only into the ear of some fool, can never happen to what is written for a whole continent. There will be a good auditor somewhere, and the farther off, the more encouraging. When your sister or your neighbor praises your work, they may be suspected of partiality; when the newspapers commend, the critic may be very friendly or very juvenile; but when the post brings you a complimentary letter from a new-born village in Colorado, you become conscious of an audience. Now, suppose the intellectual aspirations of that frontier village to be so built up by schools, libraries, and galleries that it shall be a centre of thought and civilization for the whole of Colorado, — a State which is in itself about the size of Great Britain or Italy, and half the size of Germany or France, — and we

shall have a glimpse at a state of things worth
more than a national metropolis. The collective judgment of a series of smaller tribunals
like this will ultimately be worth more to an
author, or to a literature, than that of London
or Paris. History gives us, in the Greek
states, the Italian Republics, the German university towns, some examples of such a concur-
rent intellectual jurisdiction; but they missed
the element of size, the element of democratic
freedom, the element of an indefinite future.
All these are ours.

X

THE EQUATION OF FAME

THE aim of all criticism is really to solve
the equation of fame and to find what literary work is of real value. For convenience,
the critic assumes the attitude of infallibility.
He really knows better in his own case, being
commonly an author also. The curious thing
is that, by a sort of comity of the profession,
the critic who is an author assumes that other
critics are infallible also, or at least a body
worthy of vast deference. He is as sensitive to
the praise or blame of his contemporaries as he
would have them toward himself. He bows his
head before the "London Press" or the "New
York Press" as meekly as if he did not know
full well that these august bodies are made up
of just such weak and unstable mortals as he
knows himself to be. At the Saville Club in
London an American is introduced to some
beardless youth, and presently, when some
slashing criticism is mentioned, in the *Academy*

or the *Saturday Review*, the fact incidentally comes out that his companion happened to write that very article. "Never again," the visitor thinks, "shall I be any more awed by what I read in those periodicals than if it had appeared in my village newspaper at home." But he goes his way, and in a month is looking with as much deference as ever for the "verdict of the London Press." It seems a tribute to the greatness of our common nature that the most ordinary individuals have weight with us as soon as there are enough of them to get together in a jury-box, or even in a newspaper office, and pronounce a decision. As Chancellor Oxenstiern sent the young man on his travels to see with how little wisdom the world was governed, so it is worth while for every young writer to visit New York or London, that he may see with how little serious consideration his work will be criticised. The only advantage conferred by added years in authorship is that one learns this lesson a little better, though the oldest author never learns it very well.

But apart from all drawbacks in the way of haste and shallowness, there is a profounder

difficulty which besets the most careful critical
work. It inevitably takes the color of the
time; its study of the stars is astrology, not
astronomy, to adopt Thoreau's distinction.
Heine points out, in his essay on German
Romanticism, that we greatly err in supposing
that Goethe's early fame bore much comparison
with his deserts. He was, indeed, praised for
"Werther" and "Götz von Berlichingen," but
the romances of August La Fontaine were in
equal demand, and the latter, being a volu-
minous writer, was much more in men's mouths.
The poets of the period were Wieland and
Ramler; and Kotzebue and Iffland ruled the
stage. Even forty years ago, I remember well,
it was considered an open subject of discussion
whether Goethe or Schiller was the greater
name; and Professor Felton of Harvard University took the pains to translate a long history of German literature by Menzel, the one
object of which was to show that Goethe was
quite a secondary figure, and not destined to
any lasting reputation. It was one of the
objections to Margaret Fuller, in the cultivated
Cambridge circle of that day, that she spoke

disrespectfully of Menzel in the *Dial*, and called him a Philistine — the first introduction into English, so far as I know, of that word since familiarized by Arnold and others.

We fancy France to be a place where, if governments are changeable, literary fame, fortified by academies, rests on sure ground. But Théophile Gautier, in the preface to his "Les Grotesques," says just the contrary. He declares that in Paris all praise or blame is overstated, because, in order to save the trouble of a serious opinion, they take up one writer temporarily in order to get rid of the rest. "There are," he goes on, "strange fluctuations in reputations, and auréoles change heads. After death, illuminated foreheads are extinguished and obscure brows grow bright. Posterity means night for some, dawn to others." Who would to-day believe, he asks, that the obscure writer Chapelain passed for long years as the greatest poet, not alone of France, but the whole world (*le plus grand poëte, non-seulement de France, mais du monde entier*), and that nobody less potent than the Duchesse de Longueville would have dared to go to sleep

over his poem of "*La Pucelle*"? Yet this was
in the time of Corneille, Racine, Molière, and
La Fontaine.

Heine points out that it is not enough for
a poet to utter his own sympathies, he must also
reach those of his audience. The audience, he
thinks, is often like some hungry Bedouin Arab
in the desert, who thinks he has found a sack
of pease and opens it eagerly; but, alas! they
are only pearls! With what discontent did
the audience of Emerson's day inspect his pre-
cious stones! Even now Matthew Arnold
shakes his head over them and finds Longfellow's little sentimental poem of "The Bridge"
worth the whole of Emerson. When we consider that Byron once accepted meekly his own
alleged inferiority to Rogers, and that Southey
ranked himself with Milton and Virgil, and
only with half-reluctant modesty placed himself below Homer; that Miss Anna Seward and
her contemporaries habitually spoke of Hayley
as "the Mighty Bard," and passed over without
notice Hayley's eccentric dependant, William
Blake; that but two volumes of Thoreau's writings were published, greatly to his financial

loss, during his lifetime, and eight others, with four biographies of him, since his death; that Willis's writings came into instant acceptance, while Hawthorne's, according to their early publisher, attracted "no attention whatever;" that Willis indeed boasted to Longfellow of making ten thousand dollars a year by his pen, when Longfellow wished that he could earn one-tenth of that amount, — we must certainly admit that the equation of fame may require many years for its solution. Fuller says in his "Holy State" that "learning hath gained most by those books on which the printers have lost;" and if this is true of learning, it is far truer of that incalculable and often perplexing gift called genius.

Young Americans write back from London that they wish they had gone there in the palmy days of literary society — in the days when Dickens and Thackeray were yet alive, and when Tennyson and Browning were in their prime, instead of waiting until the present period, when Rider Haggard and Oscar Wilde are regarded, they say, as serious and important authors. But just so men looked

back in longing from that earlier day to the
period of Scott and Wordsworth, and so farther
and farther and farther. It is easy for older
men to recall when Thackeray and Dickens
were in some measure obscured by now forgotten contemporaries, like Harrison Ainsworth
and G. P. R. James, and when one was gravely
asked whether he preferred Tennyson to Sterling or Trench or Alford or Faber or Milnes.
It is to me one of the most vivid reminiscences
of my Harvard College graduation (in 1841)
that, having rashly ventured upon a commencement oration whose theme was "Poetry in an
Unpoetical Age," I closed with an urgent appeal to young poets to "lay down their Spenser
and Tennyson," and look into life for themselves. Prof. Edward T. Channing, then the
highest literary authority in New England,
paused in amazement with uplifted pencil over
this combination of names. "You mean," he
said, "that they should neither defer to the
highest authority nor be influenced by the
lowest?" When I persisted, with the zeal of
seventeen, that I had no such meaning, but
regarded them both as among the gods, he said

good-naturedly, "Ah! that is a different thing.
I wish you to say what you think. I regard
Tennyson as a great calf, but you are entitled
to your own opinion." The oration met with
much applause at certain passages, including
this one; and the applause was just, for these
passages were written by my elder sister,
who had indeed suggested the subject of the
whole address. But I fear that its only value
to posterity will consist in the remark it elicited from the worthy professor; this comment
affording certainly an excellent milestone for
Tennyson's early reputation.

It is worth while to remember, also, that
this theory of calfhood, like most of the early
criticisms on Tennyson, had a certain foundation in the affectations and crudities of these
first fruits, long since shed and ignored. That
was in the period of the two thin volumes,
with their poem on the author's room, now
quotable from memory only: —

> " Oh, darling room, my heart's delight!
> Dear room, the apple of my sight!
> With thy two couches soft and white,
> There is no room so exquisite,
> No little room so warm and bright,
> Wherein to read, wherein to write."

I do not count it to the discredit of my mentor, after the lapse of half a century, that he discerned in this something which it is now the fashion to call "veal." Similar lapses helped to explain the early under-estimate of the Lake school of poets in England, and Margaret Fuller's early criticisms on Lowell. On the other hand, it is commonly true that authors temporarily elevated, in the first rude attempts to solve the equation of fame, have afforded some reason, however inadequate, for their over-appreciation. Théophile Gautier, in the essay already quoted, says that no man entirely dupes his epoch, and there is always some basis for the shallowest reputations, though what is truly admirable may find men insensible for a time. And Joubert, always profounder than Gautier, while admitting that popularity varies with the period (*la vogue des livres dépend du goût des siècles*), tells us also that only what is excellent is held in lasting memory (*la mémoire n'aime que ce qui est excellent*), and winds up his essay on the qualities of the writer with the pithy motto, "Excel and you will live" (*excelle et tu vivras*)!

XI

CONCERNING HIGH-WATER MARKS

IN Eckermann's conversations with Goethe, the poet is described as once showing his admirer a letter from Zelter which was obviously witten in a fortunate hour. Pen, paper, handwriting, were all favorable; so that for once, Goethe said, there was a true and complete expression of the man, and perhaps one never again to be obtained in like perfection. The student of literature is constantly impressed with the existence of these single autographs, these high-water marks as it were, of individual genius.

"It is in the perfection and precision of the instantaneous line," wrote Ruskin in his earlier days, "that the claim of immortality is made." Dr. Holmes somewhere counsels a young author to be wary of the fate that submerges so many famous works, and advises him to risk his all upon a small volume of poems, among which there may be one, conceived in some happy hour, that shall live. After the few great reputations there is perhaps no better anchorage in the vast sea of fame than a single sonnet like that of Blanco White. Since, at the best, one's reputation is to be determined by one's high-water mark, why not be content with that alone? If all but the one best work must surely be forgotten, why should the rest be called into existence? Let it perish with prize poems and Commencement orations, if one can only determine in advance which is the single and felicitous offspring possessing that precise quality which the physicians name " viability " — the capacity to keep itself alive.

Happily, this is not so difficult as one might suppose. It often takes a great while to determine the comparative merit of authors, — indeed, the newspapers are just now saying that the late Mr. Tupper had a larger income from the sales of his works than Browning, Tennyson, and Lowell jointly received, — but it does not take so long to determine which among an author's works are the best; and it is probable that the " Descent of Neptune " in the Iliad, and the " Vision of Helen " in the Aga-

memnon of Æschylus, and Sappho's famous
ode, and the " Birds " of Aristophanes, and the
" Hylas " of Theocritus, and the " Sparrow " of
Catullus, and the " De Arte Poetica " of
Horace were early recognized as being the
same distinct masterpieces that we now find
them. It is the tradition that an empress wept
when Virgil recited his "Tu Marcellus eris;"
and it still remains the one passage in the
Æneid that calls tears to the eye. After all,
contemporary criticism is less trivial than we
think. "Philosophers," says Novalis, "are the
eternal Nile-gauges of a tide that has passed
away, and the only question we ask of them is,
' How high water?'" But contemporary criticism is also a Nile-gauge, and it records high-
water marks with a curious approach to
accuracy.

There was never a time, for instance, when
Holmes's early poem, "The Last Leaf," was not
recognized as probably his best, up to the time
when "The Chambered Nautilus" superseded
it, and took its place unequivocally as his
high-water mark. At every author's reading
it is the crowning desire that Holmes should

read the latter of these two poems, though he is still permitted to add the former. From the moment when Lowell read his " Commemoration Ode " at Cambridge. that great poem took for him the same position; while out of any hundred critics ninety-nine would place the " Day in June " as the best of his shorter passages, and the " Bigelow Papers," of course, stand collectively for his humor. Emerson's " The Problem " — containing the only verses by a living author hung up for contemplation in Westminster Abbey — still stands as the high-water mark of his genius, although possibly, so great is the advantage possessed by a shorter poem, it may be superseded at last by his " Daughters of Time." No one doubts that Bayard Taylor will go down to fame, if at all, by his brief " Legend of Balaklava," and Julia Ward Howe by her " Battle Hymn of the Republic." It is, perhaps, characteristic of the even and well-distributed muse of Whittier that it is less easy to select his high-water mark; but perhaps " My Playmate " comes as near to it as anything. Bryant's " Waterfowl " is easily selected, and so is Longfellow's " Wreck of the

' Hesperus,' " as conveying more sense of shap-
ing imagination than any other, while " Evan-
geline " would, of course, command the majority
of votes among his longer poems.   In some
cases, as in Whitman's " My Captain," the
high-water mark may have been attained precisely at the moment when the poet departed
from his theory and confined himself most nearly
to the laws he was wont to spurn — in this case,
by coming nearest to a regularity of rhythm.

The praise generally bestowed on the admirable selections in the " Library of American
Literature," by Mr. Stedman and Miss Hutchinson, is a proof that there is a certain consensus of opinion on this subject.   Had they
left out Austin's " Peter Rugg," or Hale's " A
Man Without a Country," there would have
been a general feeling of discontent.   It would
have been curious to see if, had these editors
been forced by public opinion to put in something of their own, they would have inserted
what others would regard as their high-water
mark.   I should have predicted that it would
be so; and that this would be, in Stedman's
case, the stanzas beginning —

    " Thou art mine; thou hast given thy word,"

and closing with that unsurpassed poetic symbol of hopeless remoteness —

> " As the pearl in the depths of the sea
> From the portionless king who would wear it."

In the case of Miss Hutchinson, her exquisite little poem of " The Moth-Song " will be equally unmistakable. When Harriet Prescott Spofford's first youthful story, " Sir Rohan's Ghost," originally appeared, Lowell selected from it with strong admiration, in the *Atlantic Monthly*, the song, "In a Summer Evening;" and it still remains the most unequivocal product of her rare but unequal genius. The late Helen Jackson placed the poem called " Spinning " at the head of her volume of " Verses," not because it was that which touched the greatest depths, but because it seemed to be universally accepted as her fullest, maturest, and most thoughtful product. Aldrich's noble Fredericksburg sonnet, in a somewhat similar way, stands out by itself; it seems to differ in kind rather than degree from the " airy rhyme " of which he is wont to be the " enamored architect; " its texture is so firm, its cadence so grand, that it seems more and more likely to rank as being, next to Lowell's Ode, the most remarkable poem called out by the Civil War. It is such writing as Keats pronounced to be " next to fine doing, the top thing in the universe;" and we must not forget that Wolfe, before Quebec, pronounced fine writing to be the greater thing of the two.

The crowning instances of high-water marks are in those poems which, like Blanco White's sonnet, alone bear the writer's name down to posterity. How completely the truculent Poe fancied that he had extinguished for all time the poetry of my gifted and wayward kinsman, Ellery Channing; and yet it is not at all certain that the one closing line of Channing's " A Poet's Hope," —

" If my bark sinks, 'tis to another sea,"

may not secure the immortality it predicts, and perhaps outlive everything of Poe's. Wasson's fine poem, " Bugle Notes," beginning, —

"Sweet-voicèd Hope, thy fine discourse
    Foretold not half Life's good to me,"

will be, unless I greatly mistake, as lasting as the seventeenth-century poems among which it naturally ranks. The mere title, " Some Lover's Clear Day," of Weiss's poem will endure, perhaps, after the verses themselves and all else connected with that unique and wayward personality are forgotten. It is many years since I myself wrote of " that rare and unappreciated thinker, Brownlee Brown;" and he is less known now than he was then; yet his poem on Immortality, preserved by Stedman and Hutchinson, is so magnificent that it cheapens most of its contemporary literature, and seems alone worth a life otherwise obscure. It is founded on Xenophon's well-known story of the soldiers of Cyrus's expedition. " As soon as the men who were in the vanguard had climbed the hill and beheld the sea, they gave a great shout . . . crying ' *Thalatta! Thalatta!* ' "

THE CRY OF THE TEN THOUSAND.

" I stand upon the summit of my life:
    Behind, the camp, the court, the field, the grove,
    The battle and the burden; vast, afar,
    Beyond these weary ways, Behold, the Sea!
    The sea o'erswept by clouds and winds and wings,
    By thoughts and wishes manifold, whose breath
    Is freshness, and whose mighty pulse is peace.
    Palter no question of the horizon dim, —
    Cut loose the bark; such voyage itself is rest,
    Majestic motion, unimpeded scope,

A widening heaven, a current without care,
Eternity! — deliverance, promise, course!
Time-tired souls salute thee from the shore."

Who knows but that, when all else of American literature has vanished into forgetfulness, some single little masterpiece like this may remain to show the high-water mark, not merely of a single poet, but of a nation and a generation?

XII

PERSONAL IDEALS

SIR EDWIN ARNOLD, like most English-men of conservative proclivities, thinks that we should be better off if we had in this country a better supply of "class distinctions." He thinks that these distinctions supply to Englishmen " respect for authority and certain personal ideals which they follow devotedly." There is, no doubt, something to be said in defence of respect for authority, but everything depends upon the selection of the source. As a rule, the rich, the contented, the prosperous, think that the authority should be their own or that of their friends. The poor, the obscure, the discontented, are less satisfied with this assignment. Now it is useless to say that authority in itself is a good thing without reference to its origin or its quality. It is like saying that scales and weights are a good thing, without reference to the question who fixed their value. If you weigh by the scales of a cheating pedler, then the more authority you assign to his weights, the worse for you; better guess at it or measure out by the handful. We read in Knickerbocker's *New York* that the standard weight of the early settlers in dealing with the Indians was the weight of a Dutchman's foot; and no doubt the Indians were told that it was their duty to pay reverence to this form of authority. In England at the present day the authority is not vested in the foot of a Dutchman, but in the coronet of a German; there seems no other difference. A word from the Prince of Wales in London determines not merely the cut of a livery or the wearing of a kid glove, but the good repute of an artist or the bad repute of an actress. If he beckons a poet across the room, the poet feels honored. Indeed, the late Mrs. George Bancroft, a keen observer, once told me that she never knew an Englishman, however eminent in art or science, who, if he had dined with a duke, could help mentioning the fact to all his acquaintances. But is there anything ennobling in this form of social authority?

Now that the human race has reached some degree of maturity and self-respect, there is no dignity in any tribunal of authority except that which a self-governing nation has created for itself. Such deference, and such alone, is manly. To find such deference at its highest point, we must look for it in that entertained by the American people for its own higher courts — courts which it has created, and could at any period with a little delay abolish, but which it recognizes meanwhile as supreme authority. This same sentiment has never in our day been brought to a test so difficult and a result so triumphant as in 1876, when President Hayes was declared Chief Magistrate. Nearly one-half of the American voters honestly believed at that time that they had been defrauded of their rights; but the decision was made by a court expressly constituted for the purpose, and when made, the decree was self-executing, not a soldier being ordered out in its support. It is hard to imagine, and perhaps not desirable to see, a respect for authority more complete than this; for even such respect may be too excessive — as many of us discov-

ered during the fugitive-slave period — and may
destroy the very liberties it seeks to preserve.

When it comes to personal ideals, again,
it makes all the difference in the world whether
the ideals are to be of the genuine kind, or
merely composed of a court dress and a few
jewels. There is something noble in the reverence for an ideal, even if the object of reverence be ill-selected. There is a fine passage
in Heine's fragmentary papers on England,
where he suddenly comes, among the London
docks, to a great ship just from some Oriental
port, breathing of the gorgeous East, and
manned with a crew of dark Mohammedans of
many tribes. Weary of the land around him,
and yearning for the strange world from which
they came, he yet could not utter a word of
their language, till at last he thought of a mode
of greeting. Stretching forth his hands reverently, he cried, " Mohammed! " Joy flashed
over their dark faces, and assuming a reverent
posture, they answered, " Bonaparte! " It matters not whether either of these heroes was a
false prophet, he stood for a personal ideal, such
as no mere king or nobleman can represent;

and such an influence may exist equally under
any government. Beaconsfield and Gladstone,
Cleveland and Blaine, represent hosts of sincere
and unselfish admirers, and, on the other hand,
of bitter opponents. If the enthusiasm be
greater in England, so is the hostility; no
American statesman, not even Jefferson or
Jackson, ever was the object of such utter and
relentless execration as was commonly poured
on Gladstone in England a year or two ago in
what is called " the best society," where Sir
Edwin Arnold's ideals are supposed to be most
prevalent.

No class distinctions can do anything but
obscure such ideals as this. The habit of personal reverence — such reverence, for instance,
as the college boy gives to a favorite teacher —
is not only independent of all social barriers,
but makes them trivial. I remember that, some
ten years ago, when I was travelling by rail
within sight of Princeton College, a young
fellow next me pointed it out eagerly, and said
to me, " I suppose that there are in that college
two of the very greatest thinkers of modern
times." I asked their names, knowing that one

of them would, of course, be Dr. McCosh, and
receiving as the other name that of a gentleman ·
of whom I had never heard, and whom I have
now forgotten; so that my young friend's compliment may be distributed for what it is
worth among all those professors who may wish
to claim it. Such and so honorable was the
enthusiastic feeling expressed by President
Garfield toward Mark Hopkins, — that to sit on
the same log with him was to be in a university,— or the feeling that the Harvard students
of forty years since had toward James Walker.
Compare this boyish enthusiasm with the delight of Sir Walter Scott over the possession
of a wineglass out of which George IV. had
drunk when Prince Regent; and remember how
he carried it home for an heirloom in his family, and sat down on it and broke it after his
arrival. Which was the more noble way of
getting at a personal ideal? " There is no
stronger satire on the proud English society of
that day," says Thackeray, " than that they
admired George." When the history of this
age comes to be written by some critic as fear-
less as the author of " The Four Georges," does

any one doubt that the present Prince of Wales
— whom even *Punch* once represented as following in the steps of his uncle, like Hamlet
following the ghost, with " Go on! I'll follow
thee " — will shift his position as hopelessly as
did George the Fourth? " Which was the
most splendid spectacle ever witnessed," asks
Thackeray, " the opening feast of Prince George
in London, or the resignation of Washington?"
After all, it seems, the most eminent of modern English literary men has to turn from a
monarchy to a republic to find a splendid spectacle.

XIII

ON THE NEED OF A BACKGROUND

MR. R. W. GILDER, in a recent valuable address at Wesleyan University, gives a list of nearly a score of younger American writers, who owe, as he points out, little or nothing to the college; but he leaves the question still open whether it might not be better for some of them if they had owed the college a little more. Most of those whom he names are writers of fiction, an art in which, as in poetry, the spark of original genius counts for almost everything, and what is called literary training for comparatively little. But poetry and fiction do not constitute the whole of literature. The moment the novelist leaves the little world of his own creating and ventures on the general ground of literary production, the moment he undertakes to write history or philosophy or criticism, he feels the need of something besides creative power, something which may be called a literary background. His readers,

at any rate, demand for him, if he does not
perceive the need of it for himself, that there
shall be something which suggests a wide and
flexible training, with large vistas of knowledge. They like to see in him that " full man "
who is made, as Lord Bacon says, by "reading."

One main reason why Homer and Plato and
Horace and even Dante seem to supply more of
this kind of fulness than can be got from an
equivalent study of Balzac and Ruskin, is
doubtless because the older authors are remoter,
and so make the vista look more wide. The
vaster the better; but there must be enough of
it, at least, to convey a distinct sensation of
background. Of course, when this background
obtrudes itself into the foreground, it becomes
intolerable; and such books as Burton's "Anatomy of Melancholy" are tiresome, because they
are all made up of background, and that of the
craggiest description; but, after all, the books
which offer only foreground are also insufficient.
I do not see how any one can read the essays of
Howells and James and Burroughs, for instance,
after reading those of Emerson or Lowell or
Thoreau, without noticing in the younger trio

a somewhat narrowed range of allusion and illustration; a little deficiency in that mellow richness of soil which can be made only out of the fallen leaves of many successive vegetations; a want, in fact, of background.

It is to be readily admitted that there is no magic in a college, and that any writer who has a vast love of knowledge may secure his background for himself, as did, for example, Theodore Parker. Yet he cannot obtain it without what is, in some sense, the equivalent of a college; long early years spent in various studies, and especially in those liberal pursuits formerly known as the Humanities. No doubt there is much material accessible in other ways, as by wide travel, or even in the forecastle or on a ranch. But, after all, the main preservative of knowledge is in the art of printing; and while the merely bookish man may never make a writer, there is nothing that so enriches prose-writing as some background of book-knowledge. In case of old Burton, just mentioned, the book-knowledge clearly mastered the man; and the same is the case with one who might perhaps have been the most

fascinating of modern English authors had not
his own library proved too much for him — the
Roman Catholic Digby.   The inability to cope
with his own knowledge has been in his case
fatal to renown; his "Broad Stone of Honor"
is known to many a lover of good books in
America; yet when I was trying to find him in
London, I discovered that Froude had never
even heard his name.   It is the Nemesis of
learning; a man who cannot cope with his own
attainments is like the Norse giant who was
suffocated by his own wisdom and had to be
relieved by a siphon.   But even he may help
others, whereas the man who writes without a
background of knowledge gives but a superficial aid to anybody, although his personality
considered as a mere foreground may be very
charming.

When the writers of Oriental sacred books
began with the creation of the world, they
undoubtedly went too far for a background;
it was also going too far when the House of
Commons was more displeased by a false Latin
quantity than by a false argument.   I am perfectly willing to concede that much time has

been wasted, in times past, on the niceties of classical scholarship; and, moreover, that what is most valuable in Greek and Roman literature has been so transfused into the modern literatures that it is no longer so important as formerly to seek it at the fountain-head. It seems only a fine old-fashioned whim when we read of the desire of Dr. Popkin, the old Greek Professor at Harvard College, to retire from teaching and " read the authors," meaning thereby the Greeks alone. The authors who are worth reading have now increased to a number that would quite dismay the good professor; but the more one has read, the better for his literary background. It is necessary to use the past tense, for the need must commonly have been supplied in early life; and this implies either a college or its equivalent; that is, a period when one reads voraciously, without any limitation but in the number of hours in the day, and without any immediate necessity of literary production.

One sees but few men — I can claim to have personally known but one, the historian, Francis Parkman — for whom a perfectly well-defined literary purpose has shaped itself in early years and has proved the adequate task of a lifetime. This is not ordinarily to be expected, or even desired. Some men simply fill in a wide background without the possibility of predicting where the foreground of their intellectual work will lie. No matter; they may at any moment reap the advantage of this early breadth. There are no departments of study which are more apt to prove useful in the end than those on which Time has for a while set up the sign *No Thoroughfare.* It has been said that no one is rich in knowledge who cannot afford to let two-thirds of it lie fallow; nor can any one tell in which particular field he may at any moment be called on to resume production, or, at least, to take the benefit of some early harvest that was merely ploughed in.

While I am therefore proud, as an American, of the clever writing and even of the genius of many of the authors who owe nothing to colleges; and while I rejoice to see it demonstrated as has been shown by Mr. Howells and Mr. James, that much of the strength and delicacy of English style can be attained without early academic training; I think that it is unsafe to let our criticism stop here. We need the advantage of the background; the flavor of varied cultivation; the depth of soil that comes from much early knowledge of a great many books. This does not involve pedantry, although it is possible to be pedantic even in fiction, as Victor Hugo's endless and tiresome soliloquizers show. The deeper the sub-soil is, the more diligently the farmer must break it up; he must not prefer a shallower loam to save trouble in ploughing. The two things must be combined, — intellectual capital and labor; accumulation and manipulation; background and foreground. Addison's fame rests partly on the three folio volumes of materials which he collected before beginning the *Spectator;* but it rests also on the lightness of touch that made him Addison.

XIV

UNNECESSARY APOLOGIES

THE newspaper critics seem to me mistaken in attributing the favorable reception of Mr. Bryce's admirable book on the " American Commonwealth " to a diminished national sensitiveness. It is certain that this sensitiveness has greatly diminished, and certain also that Mr. Bryce gives us plenty of praise. But the main difference seems to lie in this, that Mr. Bryce treats us as a subject for serious study, and not as a primary class for instruction in the rudiments of morals and grammar. The usual complaint made by us against English writers is the same now as in the days of Dickens, that they come here chiefly to teach and not to inquire. No man had so many foreign visitors in his time as the late Professor Longfellow, and there never lived a man in whom the element of kindly charity more prevailed; yet he records in his diary [1] his surprise that so few foreigners apparently desire any information about this country, while all have much to communicate on the subject. The reason why every one reads with pleasure even the censures of Mr. Bryce is because he has really taken the pains to learn something about us. There is probably no American author who has traversed this continent so widely and repeatedly; there is perhaps no one who has made so careful a comparative study of the State governments; and there is certainly no one who could re-enforce this comparison by so careful a study of popular government in other times and places. To say that his book will supersede De Tocqueville is to say little; it is better for the present period than was De Tocqueville for any period; because it is as clear, as candid, and incomparably more thorough.

All this refers to the main theme of Mr. Bryce's book; but there is one criticism yet to be made upon it. It is to be regretted that he was ever tempted from his main ground, where he is so strong, to a collateral ground, where

[1] January 16, 1845.

he is weaker. It was not, perhaps, necessary that he should treat of American literature at all; at any rate, it is safe to say that his chapter on this subject has a perfunctory air; it seems like the work of a tired man, who feels that he ought to say something on that point, yet does not care to grapple with it as with his main question; and so puts us off with vague and needless, though kindly apologies. He is so ready to find good reasons for our doing no more, that he takes no pains to analyze or weigh what we have done; and unfortunately the habit of colonial deference is still so strong among us, that we are more disposed to be grateful to such a kindly apologist than to question his words. It has been a lifelong conviction with me that the injury done to American literature by the absence of a copyright law is a trivial thing compared with the depressing influence of this prolonged attitude of dependence: an attitude which has disappeared from our political institutions, but still exists in regard to books. To test it we have only to reverse in imagination the nationality of a few authors and critics, and consider what a change of estimate such an altered origin would involve. Let us make, for instance, the great effort of supposing Emerson an English author and Matthew Arnold an American; does any one suppose that Arnold's criticisms on Emerson would in that case have attracted very serious attention in either country? Had Mr. Gosse been a New Yorker, writing in a London magazine, would any one on either side of the Atlantic have seriously cared whether Mr. Gosse thought that contemporary England had produced a poet? The reason why the criticisms of these two Englishmen have attracted such widespread notice among us is that they have the accumulated literary weight — the *ex oriente lux* — of London behind them. We accept them meekly and almost reverently; just as we even accept the criticisms made on Grant and Sheridan by Lord Wolseley, who is, compared to either of these generals, but a carpet knight. It is in some such way that we must explain the meek gratitude with which our press receives it, when Mr. Bryce apologizes for our deficiencies in the way of literature.

Mr. Bryce — whom, it is needless to say, I

regard with hearty admiration, and I can add
with personal affection, since he has been my
guest and I have been his — Mr. Bryce has a
chapter on " Creative Intellectual Power," in
which he has some capital remarks on the impossibility of saying why great men appear in
one time or place and not in another — in
Florence, for instance, and not in Naples or
Milan.   Then he goes on to say that there is
" no reason why the absence of brilliant genius
among the sixty millions in the United States
should excite any surprise," and adds soon
after, "It is not to be made a reproach against
America that men like Tennyson or Darwin
have not been born there."   Surely not; nor
is it a reproach against England that men like
Emerson or Hawthorne have not been born
there.   But if this last is true, why did it not
occur to Mr. Bryce to say it; and had he said
it, is it not plain that the whole tone and statement of his proposition would have been different?   It occurs to him to specify Darwin and
Tennyson, but the two men who above all
others represent creative intellectual power, up
to this time, in America, are not so much as
named in his whole chapter of thirteen pages.

Of course it is too early for comparison, but it is undoubtedly the belief of many Americans — at any rate, it is one which I venture to entertain — that the place in the history of intellect held a hundred years hence by the two Americans he forgets to mention will be greater than that of the two Englishmen he names. Greater than Darwin's, from the more lasting quality of literary than of scientific eminence. Darwin was great, as he was certainly noble and lovable; but he was not greater, or at least held greater, than Newton: —

> " Nature and Nature's laws lay hid in night,
> God said, ' Let Newton be,' and all was light."

More than this could surely not be said for Darwin; and yet how vague and dim is now the knowledge, even among educated men, of precisely what it was that Newton accomplished, compared with the continued knowledge held by every school-boy as to Pope, who wrote the lines just quoted. The mere record of Darwin's own life shows how large a part of man's highest mental action became inert in him. He ceased to care for the spheres of thought in

which Emerson chiefly lived; while, on the
other hand, the tendencies and results of Darwin's thought were always an object of interest
to Emerson.

When we turn to Tennyson the comparison
must proceed on different grounds, and takes
us back to Coleridge's fine definition of inspiration, given half a century ago in his " Con-
fessions of an Inquiring Spirit." " Whatever *finds me*," he wrote, " at a greater depth
than usual, that is inspired." It is because
Emerson in his way and Hawthorne in his way
touch us at greater depths than Tennyson that
their chance for immortality is stronger. Form
is doubtless needed in the expression; but in
Hawthorne there is no defect of form, and the
frequent defects of this kind in Emerson are
balanced by tones and cadences so noble that
the exquisite lyre of Tennyson, taken at its
best, has never reached them. I do not object
to the details of treatment in Mr. Bryce's chapter, and it contains many admirable suggestions; but it seems to me that he might well
preface it, in a second edition, by some such
remark — addressed to some fancied personifica-

tion of American Literature — as Enobarbus,
in " Antony and Cleopatra," makes to Pom-
pey : —

" Sir,
I never loved you much: but I have praised you
When you have well deserved ten times as much
As I have said you did."

XV

THE PERILS OF AMERICAN HUMOR

NOTHING strikes an American more, on his first visit to England, than the frequent discussion of American authors who are rarely quoted at home, except in stump-speeches, and whose works hardly have a place as yet in our literary collections, and who still are taken seriously among educated persons in England. The astonishment increases when he finds the almanacs of "Josh Billings" reprinted in "Libraries of American Humor," and given an equal place with the writings of Holmes and Lowell. Finally he is driven to the conclusion that there must be very little humor in England, where things are seriously published in book form which here would only create a passing smile in the corner of a newspaper. He finds that the whole department of American humor was created, so to speak, by the amazed curiosity of Englishmen. It is a phrase that one rarely hears in the United States; and

if we have such a thing among us, although it
may cling to our garments, we are habitually
as unconscious of it as are smokers of the per-
fume of their favorite weed. When attention
is once called to it, however, we are compelled
to perceive it, and may then look at it both
from the desirable and undesirable sides, since
both of these sides it has.

There is certainly no defence or water-proof
garment against adverse fortune which is, on
the whole, so effectual as an habitual sense of
humor. The man who has it can rarely be cast
down for a great while by external events; and
it is much the same with a nation. For some
reason or other, in the transplantation to this
continent, certain traits were heightened and
certain other qualities were diminished among
the English-speaking race. Thus much may
be safely assumed. Among the heightened
attributes was the sense of humor; and to this,
no doubt, some of our seeming virtues may
be attributed.

The good-nature of an American crowd, the
long-suffering of American travellers under
detention or even fraud, the recoil of cheer-

fulness after the tremendous excitement of a
national election — all these things are partly
due to the national habit of looking not so
much at the bright side as at the amusing side
of all occurrences. The day after election the
most heated partisan, beaten or victorious, not
only laughs at the other party, but he laughs
at his own; he laughs at himself; and this attitude of mind, which carried Abraham Lincoln
through the vast strain of civil war and emancipation, is an almost essential trait of life in a
republic. Public men who have this quality
are able to thrive on the very wear and tear of
political life; public men who are without it,
as the late Charles Sumner, find the path of
duty hard, and are kept up by sheer conscience
and will. And so in private life, the husband
and wife who have no mutual enjoyment of
this kind, the parents who derive no delight
from the droll side of nursery life and the perpetual unconscious humor of childhood, must
find daily existence monotonous and wearing.
It was from this point of view that one of the
cleverest and most useful women I have ever
known, the late Mrs. Delano Goddard, of

Boston, when asked what quality on the whole best promoted one's usefulness in life, replied, "The sense of humor."

But when this sense of humor is, as one may say, nationalized, it furnishes some occasional disadvantages to set against this merit. It may not only be turned against good causes, but against the whole attitude of earnest study or faithful action. Mr. Warner has lately pointed out how not merely the external reputation of Chicago has been injured, but its whole intellectual life retarded, by the determined habit of the newspapers of that city in treating all intellectual efforts coming from that quarter as a joke. "When Chicago makes up her mind to take hold of culture," said one of the local humorists, "she will just make culture hum." Of course it might seem that every word of this vigorous sentence must serve to put culture a little farther off. But, as a matter of fact, culture is already there, in Chicago. There is probably no city in the Union which publishes books of a higher grade, in proportion to their numbers. Looking on the fly-leaf of a new London edition of Sir

Philip Sidney's "Astrophel and Stella," the
other day, I was not at all surprised to find
that, of the thousand copies printed, one-
quarter were for the American market, and
that these were to be issued from Chicago.
And yet so fixed is this habit of joking in the
mind of our people that it will probably last an
indefinite period into the future, and keep all
the intellectual impulses of that particular city
in the kind of uncomfortable self-consciousness
which comes from being always on the defen-
sive. In time such an attitude is outgrown,
and people are left to enjoy what they like. I
can remember when the disposition of Bosto-
nians to take pleasure in Beethoven's sym-
phonies was almost as much of a joke to Boston
editors as is the "humming" of culture in
Chicago to-day; but there is fortunately a limit
to human endurance in regard to certain particular witticisms, though some of them certainly
die hard. .

The same necessity for a joke invades other
quiet enjoyments and harmless occupations, as
the study of Shakespeare or Browning. It has
happened to me to look in at several different

Browning clubs, first and last; but the club of
the newspaper humorist I never have happened
to encounter — that club which is as vague and
misty and wordy as that other creation of the
American imagination, the "Limekiln Club"
of colored philosophers.   On the contrary, such
Browning clubs as I have happened to look in
upon have had the sobriety and reasonableness
which are essential to the study of a poet who,
although often recondite and difficult, is never
vague.   Yet you may go to the meeting of such
a club and be struck with the good-sense and
moderation of every word that is uttered; no
matter; the report in the next day's newspaper
— if reporters are admitted — will put in all
the folly and adulation that the meeting wisely
left out, and this because the reporter is
expected to exhibit humor.   It is worse yet
when serious public discussions or the terrible
details of police courts are burlesqued in this
way.   Few things, I should say, are more
essentially demoralizing than the facetious
police report of the enterprising daily newspaper.   The moral of it all is that humor, like
fire, is a good servant but a bad master; that it

refreshes and relieves the hard work of life, and is meant to do so in the order of nature; but when it becomes an end in itself it takes the real dignity from life, and actually makes its serious work harder.

XVI

ON THE PROPOSED ABOLITION OF THE PLOT

IT was said of the romantic Muse in Germany — of the Pegasus, or winged horse of Uhland — that, like its colleague, the famous war-horse Bayard, it possessed all possible virtues and but one fault, that it was dead. It is in this decisive way that Mr. Howells and others deal with the plot in stories and dramas; they decline to argue the matter, but simply assert that the plot is extinct. If any one doubts the assertion they would perhaps still decline to argue the matter, and simply extend the assertion to any critic who differed from them, pointing out that he must be dead also. It may be so, since there may always be room for such a possibility. "Tyrawley and I," said Walpole's old statesman. "have been dead these two years; but we don't let anybody know it." In the matter of literary criticism, however, the fact is just the other way. The

critics who cling to the plot are not aware of
their own demise; but Mr. Howells has found
it out. To find it out is justly to silence them;
for, as Charles Lamb says in his poem exempli-
fying "the lapidary style," which the late Mr.
Mellish never could abide: —

> " It matters very little what Mellish said,
> Because he is dead."

But if we grant for a moment, as a matter
of argument, that whatever yet speaks may be
regarded, for controversial purposes, as being
alive, it may be well enough pointed out, that,
if plot is dead and only characters survive, then
there is a curious divergence in this age between the course of literature and the course of
science. If anything marks the science of the
age it is that plot is everything. Museums
were formerly collections of detached specimens, only classified for convenience under a
few half-arbitrary divisions. One may still see
such collections surviving, for instance, in that
melancholy hall through which people pass, as
rapidly as possible, to reach the modern theatre
known as the Boston Museum. But in all

natural history museums of any pretensions,
the individual specimen is subordinated to the
whole. The great Agassiz collection at Harvard is expressly named "The Museum of Comparative Zoölogy." In the Peabody Museum at
Yale — in which, as Charles Darwin told me,
quoting Huxley, there is more to be learned
than from all the museums of Europe — you are
not shown the skeleton of a horse, and left with
that knowledge, but you are shown every step
in the development of the horse from the time
when, in pre-historic periods, he was no larger
than a fox and had five toes. In science, plot
is not only not ignored, but it is almost everything; only it is not called plot, it is called
evolution.

And conversely, what is called evolution in
science is called plot in fiction. Grant that
character is first in importance, as it doubtless
is, yet plot is the development of character. It
is not enough to paint Arthur Dimmesdale,
standing with his hand on his heart and despair
in his eyes; to paint the hand anatomically
correct, the eyes deep in emotion; but we need
to know what brought him there; what pro-

duced the strange combination, a Puritan Saint with a conscience wrung into distortion. Lear is not Lear, Hamlet not Hamlet, without a glimpse at the conditions that have made them what they are. With the worst villains of the play, we need, as Margaret Fuller profoundly said, to "hear the excuses men make to themselves for their worthlessness." But these conditions, these excuses, constitute the plot.

It is easy enough to dismiss plot from the scene, if it means only a conundrum like that in "The Dead Secret," or a series of riddles like the French detective novels. In these the story is all, there is no character worth unravelling; and when we have once got at the secret the book is thrown away. But where the plot is a profound study of the development of character, it can never be thrown away; and unless we have it, the character is not really studied. What we do at any given moment is largely the accumulated result of all previous action; and that action again comes largely from the action of those around us. "We are all members one of another." Just as we are all learning this in political economy,.

are we to drop it out of view in fiction? The thought or impulse that springs into my mind or heart this instant has been largely moulded by a hundred men and women, living or dead; if the novelist or the dramatist wishes to portray me, he must include them also. Otherwise the picture is as hopelessly detached and isolated as the figure in this sketch that a very young artist has just brought me in from the seaside — a little boy standing at the apex of a solitary rock, fishing in the ocean; the whole vast sea around him, but not a living thing near him — not even a fish.

We all find ourselves, as we come into mature society and take our part in life, surrounded by a network of event and incident, one-tenth public and nine-tenths private. If we have warm hearts and observant minds we are pretty sure to be entangled in this network. By middle life, every person who has seen much of the world is acquainted with secrets that would convulse the little circle around him, if told; and might easily eclipse all the novels, if the very complication of the matter did not forbid utterance. As no painter,

it is said, ever dared paint the sunset as bright
as it often is, so the most thrilling novelist un-
derstates the mystery and entanglement in the
actual world around him. If he is cautious,
he may well say, as the Duke of Wellington
is said to have remarked when meditating his
autobiography: "I should like to speak the
truth; but if I do, I shall be torn in pieces."
If our realists would say frankly: "We should
like to draw plots such as we have actually
known; but we dare not do it, let us therefore
abolish the plot," their position would be far
more intelligible. Miss Alcott's heroine, in
writing her first stories, finds with surprise
that all the things she has taken straight from
real life are received with incredulity; and
only those drawn wholly from her internal consciousness are believed at all. Life goes so
much beyond fiction that those who are brought
up mainly on the latter diet are more apt to
encounter something in life which eclipses fiction than something which seems tame in comparison. And, on the other hand, when we
put real events into the form of fiction, they
seem over-wrought and improbable.

Much of this applies, of course, to character as well as to plot. The seeming contradictions in the character of Hamlet, over which the critics have wrangled for a century or two, are not really so great or improbable as those to be found in many youths who pass for commonplace; and that man's experience is limited who has not encountered, in his time, women of more "infinite variety" than Shakespeare's Cleopatra. Character in real life is a far more absorbing study than character in fiction; and when it comes to plot, fiction is nowhere in comparison. Toss a skein of thread into the sea. and within twenty-four hours the waves and the floating seaweed will have tangled it into a knot more perplexing than the utmost effort of your hands can weave; and so the complex plots of life are wound by the currents of life itself, not by the romancers. If life thus provides them, they are a part of life, and must not be omitted when there is a pretence at its delineation. I once heard an eloquent preacher (W. H. Channing) express the opinion that we should spend a considerable part of eternity in unravelling the strange history of one another's lives. It might be easy, perhaps, to devise more profitable ways of spending eternity; but there is no doubt that the pursuit he proposes, if we undertook it, would occupy a good many ages of that period. It would be necessary, however, to stipulate that none of it should be given to us in the form of autobiography, since we have altogether too much of that offered to us in this life. To make our friends really interesting, we must be allowed to explore their secrets in spite of them, and perhaps against their direct opposition.

Of course we all view this drama of life around us through a medium varying with our temperaments. Heine says that he once went to see the thrilling tragedy of "*La Tour de Nesle*," in Paris, and sat behind a lady who wore a large hat of rose-red gauze. The hat obstructed his whole view of the stage; he saw the play only through it, and all the horror of the tragedy was transformed by the most cheerful roselight. Some of us are happy in having this rose-tinted veil in our temperaments; but the plot and the tragedy are there. "The inno-

cent," says Thoreau speaking of life, "enjoy
the story." They should be permitted to enjoy
it, which they cannot do unless they have it.
Grant that character is the important thing;
but character will soon dwindle and its delineation grow less and less interesting, if we
detach it from life. We are all but coral-
insects or sea-anemones forming a part of one
great joint existence, and we die and dry up if
torn from the reef where we belong.

XVII

AMERICAN TRANSLATORS

THE English-speaking race has a strong instinct for translation, extending through both its branches. Miss Mitford says of one of her heroes in a country town, "He translated Horace, as all gentlemen do;" and Mrs. Austin speaks of Goethe's "Faust" as "that untranslatable poem which every Englishman translates." Americans are not behind their British cousins in these labors; and Professor Boyesen — who, as a Norseman by birth and an American by adoption, is free of all languages — has written an agreeable paper in *Book News*[1] on the general subject of translations. In this he says that America has produced three of the greatest translators of modern times; a statement which every patriotic American would perhaps indorse, were he himself only allowed to make the selection. To two out of three of Mr. Boyesen's favorites I should certainly take

[1] August, 1888.

decided objection; and, curiously enough, should nominate as substitutes two other translators of the very books he selects as test-subjects for rendering.

About Longfellow there can be no difference of opinion. He seems to me, as to Mr. Boyesen, to rank first among those who have made translations into the English tongue. He alone avoids the perpetual difference between literal and poetic versions by absolutely combining the two methods; a thing which Mr. Boyesen thinks — but, I should say, mistakenly — cannot be done. Mr. Boyesen's *dictum* that "no poetic translation can be good and literal at the same time," is refuted by the very existence of Longfellow, whose instinct for the transference of his author's language seemed like a sixth sense or a special gift for that one purpose. Placing side by side his German ballads and their originals, one neither detects anything of Longfellow put in nor anything of Uhland or Heine left out. The more powerful and commanding class of translators insert themselves into the work of their authors; thus Chapman so Chapmanizes Homer that in the long run his

version fails to give pleasure; and Fiztgerald
has whole lines in his "Agamemnon" which
are not in Æschylus and are almost indistin-
guishable in flavor from his "Omàr Kháyyàm."
Even Mrs. Austin, in that exquisite version
quoted by Longfellow in his "Hyperion,"
beginning

"Many a year is in its grave,"

has infused into it a tinge of dreamy sentiment
slightly beyond that conveyed by Uhland in the
original.

It is perhaps more beautiful, as it stands,
than any of Longfellow's ballad-versions; but
it is less perfect as a rendering. It is ·possible
that Longfellow's own method swerved a little,
in his later years, toward over-literalness.
There are many who prefer the freer and more
graceful movement of his "Vision of Beatrice"
in the "Ballads and other Poems" to the
stricter measure of the same passage in his com-
pleted translation. This last work has truly,
as Mr. Boyesen says, an air of constraint; but
I think he is in error in attributing this quality
to the influence of those who met to criticise

Longfellow's work; it was rather due to the strong hold taken, by the theory of a literal rendering, on the poet's mind. Over-literalness appears to be the Nemesis of a genius for translating; the longer a man works, the more precise he becomes.

The second of Mr. Boyesen's great American translators is Bryant; and here I should utterly dissent from him. The best introduction to Homer in English is Matthew Arnold's "Essay on Translating Homer;" or rather it would be, but for its needless and diffuse length, which prevents many persons from really mastering it; but I do not see how any one, after reading it, can look through a page of Bryant's version without a sense of its utter tameness and its want of almost all the qualities defined by Arnold as essential to Homer. Mr. Lawton has finely said, at the beginning of his admirable papers on Æschylus in the *Atlantic Monthly* [1] that "the Homeric poems offer us, as it were, a glimpse of a landscape scene by a flash of lightning. What came before and immediately after we cannot discern." But in

[1] August, 1888.

Bryant's translation there is substituted for the flash of lightning the very mildest moonlight; and there seems no particular reason, from anything in the tone or flavor of his narrative, why the whole series of events should not have taken place on Staten Island. Mr. Bryant undoubtedly had, in his youth, something of Longfellow's gift for translation; his early Spanish ballads had in them much promise; they were as good as Lockhart's, perhaps better. But his "Iliad" and "Odyssey" were an old man's work, done with mechanical regularity, so many lines a day; and while they are "grave and dignified," as his critic says, they are Homer with the fire of Homer — or, in other words, with Homer himself — left out. But the real translator of the Father of Poetry is, in my judgment, one whom Mr. Boyesen does not name, and perhaps does not yet know, so recently has the first instalment of his great work appeared — Prof. G. H. Palmer. For the last half-dozen years it has been the greatest intellectual pleasure afforded by a residence near Harvard University to follow with the Greek text the public readings of Professor

Palmer from the "Odyssey." These readings were given so simply, with such quiet and sustained animation, that it all seemed like an extempore performance; and all the incidents were told with such utter freshness that they might have just arrived as news by telegraph. This English text is published; it is cast, with consummate art, in a sort of rhythmic prose, perfectly simple, yet measured, and securing, perhaps, the nearest approach that can be had in English to the actual rhythm of Homer. Professor Palmer will now have to solve the further and more difficult problem, whether the stronger and richer measure of the "Iliad" can be dealt with in the same way. But the work already done is one of the monumental works of American scholarship; and although it stands to the eye as a prose version, and might at first be hastily classed with a translation so incomparably inferior to it as that of Butcher and Lang, yet it is really as literal as that, while achieving at least half the interval, whatever that may be, which separates prose from poetry.

Mr. Boyesen's third great American translator is Bayard Taylor. Here again he seems

to me to concede too much to labor and not
enough to genius. As a *tour de force*, Taylor's
great work is doubtless monumental, and an
honor to American scholarship. I remember
with what regret I noticed that there was no
copy of it, ten years ago, in the collection
of Goethean literature in the Göthe-Haus at
Frankfort, though Taylor's honorary diploma
was there, and the custodian spoke of him with
respect. As a translator of the whole work,
and as a copious commentator and elucidator
he is entitled to great credit, although his
abundant notes are taken largely from German
sources, easily accessible. No Englishman, at
any rate, has done the same work so well. But
it is to be remembered that although the translation of the Second Part of "Faust," in the
original metres, taxes severely the ingenuity
and adroitness of any workman, yet it is in
dealing with the oft-translated First Part that
the higher poetic qualities come in; and in this
Taylor has been easily surpassed, I should say,
by the late Charles T. Brooks. And while
Brooks, it is true, stopped short of the longer
and more laborious Second Part, yet he made

up for that by his remarkable series of versions of the yet more difficult work of Jean Paul Richter. These he handled, especially the "Hesperus" and "Titan," with a felicity and success unequalled among Richter's translators; and it is an illustration of the ignorance in England of the successes achieved by Americans in this direction, that Mr. Brooks's works of this series are there so little recognized. Another remarkable American translator from the German is Charles G. Leland, whose version of Heine's *Reisebilder* under the name of "Pictures of Travel" is so extraordinarily graphic and at the same time so literal that it ought of itself to achieve a permanent fame for the author of "Hans Breitmann."

XVIII

THE WESTMINSTER ABBEY OF A BOOK CATALOGUE

THE American visitor enters Westminster Abbey prepared to be hushed in awe before the multitude of great names. To his amazement he finds himself vexed and bored with the vast multiplicity of small ones. He must approach the Poets' Corner itself through avenues of. Browns, Joneses, and Robinsons. It seems that even Westminster Abbey affords no test of greatness, nor do any of the efforts to ascertain it by any other test succeed much better. The balloting in various newspapers for "the best hundred authors" or "the forty immortals" has always turned out to be limited by the constituency of the particular publication which attempted the experiment; or sometimes even by the action of jocose cliques, combining to force up the vote of pet candidates. As regards American authors, the great "Li-

brary of American Literature " of Stedman and
Hutchinson aims to furnish a sort of Westminster Abbey or Valhalla, where the relative
value of different writers may be roughly
gauged by the number of pages assigned to
each candidate for fame. But this again is
determined by the taste of the compilers, and
their judgment, however catholic, is not infallible. Still another test, and one coming nearer
to a general popular consensus may be sought
in the excellent catalogues which are now prepared for our public libraries — catalogues in
which the list of each author's works is supple-
mented by appending the titles of all books or
parts of books written about him; not usually
including, however, magazine or newspaper
articles. By simply counting the entries of
this subsidiary literature which has already
grown up around each eminent man, we can
obtain a certain rough estimate of the extent
and variety of interest inspired by him in the
public mind.

Let us take, for instance, one of the best and
most recent of these catalogues — the large
quarto volume which enumerates the English

books in the Cleveland (Ohio) public library. This selection is made partly because of the thoroughness and excellence of the work itself, and partly because, as Emerson once said, "Europe stretches to the Alleghanies," and, by going west of them, we at least rid ourselves of any possible prejudices of the Atlantic border. I have carefully counted the list of entries in this catalogue under the names of many prominent Americans not now living; and the results have been such as to surprise not merely the present writer, but all with whom he has compared notes. No person to whom he has put the question has yet succeeded in hitting, at a guess, the first four names upon the list presently to be given; the list, that is, of those under whose names the entry of biographical and critical literature is largest. The actual table, arranged in order of pre-eminence, is as follows, the number following each name representing the number of books, or parts of books, referring to the person named, and enumerated in the Cleveland catalogue. The actual works of the author himself are not included. The list is as follows: —

Washington	48
Emerson, Lincoln (each)	41
Franklin	37
Webster	34
Longfellow	33
Hawthorne	25
Jefferson	23
Grant	22
Irving	21
Clay	19
Beecher, Poe, M. F. Ossoli (each) . . .	16
Theodore Parker, Lowell (each)	15
John Adams, Sumner (each)	14
Cooper, Greeley, Sheridan, Sherman (each) .	12
Everett	11
John Brown, Channing, Farragut (each) . .	10
Garrison, Hamilton, Prescott, Seward, Taylor (each)	9
Thoreau	7
Bancroft	6
Allston	5
Edwards, Motley (each)	5

This list certainly offers to the reader some
surprises in its details, but it must impress
every one, after serious study, as giving a
demonstration of real intelligence and catho-
licity of taste in the nation whose literature it
represents. When, for instance, we consider
the vast number of log cabins or small farm-
houses where the name of Lincoln is a household
word, while that of Emerson is as unknown as

that of Æschylus or Catullus, one cannot help wondering that there should have been as many books written — so far as this catalogue indicates — about the recluse scholar as about the martyr-president. The prominence of Washington and Franklin was to be expected, but that Longfellow should come so near Webster, and that both he and Hawthorne should distinctly precede Jefferson and Grant, affords surely some sensations of surprise. Again, there is something curious in the fact that Poe should stand "bracketed," as they say of examination papers, with the Margaret Fuller whom he detested; that the classic Everett should fall so far below the radical Parker; and that Dr. Channing and John Brown, the antipodes of each other as to temperament, should rank together on the returns. But all must agree that these figures reflect, to a greater degree than one would have expected, the actual prominence of these various personages in the public mind; and could the table include a number of printed catalogues instead of one, it really would afford as fair an approximation as we are likely to obtain to a National gallery of eminent persons.

It is easily to be seen that no similar gallery of living persons would have much value. It is not, ordinarily, until after a man's death that serious criticism or biography begins. Comparing a few living names, we find that there are already, in the Cleveland catalogue, subsidiary references to certain living persons, as follows: —

Holmes, Whittier	12
Mrs. Stowe	8
Whitman	5
Ex-President Cleveland	4
Harte	3
Blaine, Howells, James	2
Hale, Parkman	1

These figures, so far as they go, exhibit the same combination of public and literary service with those previously given. Like those, they effectually dispose of the foolish tradition that republican government tends to a dull mediocrity. Here we see a people honoring by silent suffrages their National leaders, and recording the votes in the catalogue of every town library. There is no narrow rivalry between literature and statesmanship, or between either of these and military qualities, but all leaders are recognized for what they have given. The result is a tribute to that natural inequality of men which is as fully recognized, in a true republic, as their natural equality; that is, they are equal in the sense of being equally men, but not equal in their gifts as men. It is curious to see how the social falsities of English society tell on educated Englishmen, so surely as they grow old enough to shed the generous impulses of youth. It was in vain that Tennyson wrote "Clara Vere de Vere." and Froude "The Nemesis of Faith," and Ruskin "Modern Painters," and Swinburne the "Song in Time of Order:" let them once reach middle life and they are all stanch Tories and "accept dukes;" and now Huxley follows in their train. But here in America we find no difficulty in selecting our natural leaders, sooner or later, and owning them; they do not have to fight for recognition, in most cases; it comes by a process like the law of gravitation.

In our colonial town records the object of the meeting was often stated as being "to know the Town's Mind" on certain questions; the Town's

Mind being always written with capitals and
"mentioned with reverence, as if it were a distinguished person, hard to move." The result
of this unconscious selection in the book catalogues is to give us the Nation's Mind in
regard to our foremost men. As time goes
on, the decision varies; some reputations hold
out better, some less well; the relative position
of Dr. Channing, for instance, has changed
a good deal within fifty years, and so has that
of Henry Clay; but in the end the scale settles
itself and remains tolerably permanent. And
there is this advantage in a hierarchy of intellect and public service thus established, that it
does not awaken the antagonism which follows
an hereditary aristocracy; and that if the sons
of these eminent persons do not distinguish
themselves, they are simply ignored and passed
by, whereas under a hereditary aristocracy their
high position may be a curse to the community.
This Westminster Abbey of the newspapers
excites no such feelings as Heine confesses
himself to have experienced among the graves
of the crowned heads at Westminster Abbey in
London. He tells us that he did not grudge

the eighteen pence he had paid to see them; but told the verger that he was delighted with his exhibition, and would willingly have paid as much more to see the collection complete.

XIX

TOWN AND GOWN

DURING the two years when the writer was a member of a State legislature, he was often asked if he did not encounter a certain widely spread prejudice against college-bred men. Truth compelled him to reply that he did, but that it almost always proceeded from other college-bred men. Having all his life been in the habit of attending caucuses and political meetings, and having very often presided over them, he has had some opportunity of testing the alleged prejudice of the uneducated against the more educated, in a democratic community, and he can truly say that he never happened to encounter it; but he has very often encountered the attempt to create it among those who should have known better. In the close contests of politics there is often a temptation to find a weapon against an opponent in the charge of being college-bred or having written a book; but the persons who

yield to this temptation are mostly those who
have themselves suffered from a similar im-
peachment, and fancy that they can score a
point by turning States' evidence on their own
training. But I have never seen that the effort
had more than a very temporary influence in
the community at large; and this for obvious
reasons.

To begin with, there is very little of this
prejudice among the poorer classes in any
American community, for these classes are,
whether Protestants or Catholics, not yet very
remote from the time when they reverenced
their clergy, and when this body represented
leadership in all the walks of life. Among the
Puritans, as is well known, the colleges existed
to train clergymen, and the clergy existed to
fill all the posts of leadership. There was no
separate legal profession, for instance; and
Chief Justice Sewall — whose racy journals
make him the more sombre Pepys of the New
England Colonial period — was educated for
the ministry and took a seat on the bench by
way of collateral pursuit, precisely as he accepted the command of the Ancient and Honor-

able Artillery Company and paraded with it on
the Boston Common. Professor Goodale, the
Harvard botanist, has lately shown that the
beginnings of natural science in the curriculum
of that institution were due to the fact, that
being organized for the rearing of Christian
ministers it must give them some knowledge of
anatomy and the *Materia Medica*, in order that
they might prescribe for their sick parishioners.
Even business matters were to some extent
within their grasp, and this lasted into this century. An eminent lawyer, distinguished for his
skill in the charge of great trust properties, having lately died in Boston, I was calling attention to the fact that when I knew him, in college,
he never gave the slightest sign of peculiar
business aptitude; but I was at once told
by one who had known his father, a country
clergyman, that this good pastor was the business adviser of his whole parish, and did for
rural traders what his son afterward did for
great capitalists. Thus much for the Protestant side; and among our Catholic citizens it
is so the custom to see the clergy intrusted
with great financial responsibilities, that no

sneer against educated men ever comes from them; they err on the other side, in too great willingness to intrust their savings to their spiritual advisers.

The supposed prejudice against the incapacity of men of scholarly pursuits does not, therefore, come from the poorer class, whether Catholic or Protestant, nor does it come from the great intermediate and powerful class of the Silas Laphams; on the contrary, the college-bred man is more often touched by a certain covert and needless humility on the part of this class. The organizers of labor, the heads of great enterprises, are often mute and timid before those very much their inferiors in real training, simply from their consciousness that they are weak in things which are really of secondary importance. Just as an Englishman who has once discovered that he misplaces his H's will sometimes hold his tongue when he has things to say more important than all the separate letters of the alphabet put together; so is it often with the uneducated American who seems to exult in all the glory of material success. In the Massachusetts Legislature I have had men come and beg me to make their speeches for them in regard to a certain measure, they putting all the facts and material into my hands, although they knew ten times as much about it as I, and could, consequently, make a far more effective speech; and this simply because they knew that their verbs did not always agree with their nominative cases, and they attached an exaggerated importance to this minor matter. Whatever may be the defects of the much-discussed American temperament. obtuseness is certainly not one of them. The unschooled American recognizes and laments his ignorance, and, indeed, commonly exaggerates it; that is, he does not reflect that he perhaps knows things which are vastly more important than the things which he does not know, and which his college-bred neighbor knows. That is why he sends his son to college. A friend of mine, a merchant by training and a most acute observer, had a theory that the college graduates did not care so very much to send their sons where they had been, as knowing that it had not done very much for themselves; but that the non-grad-

uates were very anxious to send theirs, because
they attributed their own shortcomings to the
want of that early advantage. Thus, he
reasoned, every alternate generation goes to
the university.

In the same way, I think that the college-
bred man, or at any rate the man of literary
pursuits, is apt to be more humble for himself
than he is wished by others to be. It is like
that curious self-humiliation, at the beginning
of our Civil War, of those who had not been
trained in the militia, in presence of those who
had received such training. A book of tac-
tics looked, when one opened it, harder than
Euclid's Geometry; and it took a little time
to discover that it was, for a man with tolerably clear head, as simple as the spelling-book.
So the student is apt to think that the elementary principles of business, or the rules of par-
liamentary law, are things requiring long and
difficult training; whereas they do not, in
acquiring, prove very hard. Then it must be
remembered that, in this country at least, the
scholar has very commonly made his own way
in the world and has had to develop the prac-

tical faculty, in a small way, from the very
beginning. Nothing is more interesting, in a
university town, than to see the variety of ante-
cedents, usually involving some knowledge of
men, with which the older students have come
together. In a nation where small mechanics
and country shopkeepers become millionnaires
and presidents, it is not strange that the student
whose early life was perhaps not very different from theirs should also have his practical
side.

It must be remembered that the supposed
prejudice against educated men in practical
affairs is not confined to our own country, but
exists in England, in France, in Germany; and
in each case with the additional condition
which I have pointed out, that it is found more
among other educated men than in the general
public mind. We think of England as a place
where they put authors forward in public life;
and we instance Beaconsfield, Gladstone,
Morley, and Bryce, by way of illustration.
But the acute Sir Frederick Elliot wrote to the
poet Sir Henry Taylor, in 1876: "I think that
literati, when they have not been exercised in

practical affairs (note that exception!) are the worst of politicians." He has especially in mind historians, and makes the point, which is worth noticing, that they are a little apt to confound the dead and the living. "Look at Freeman; he digs into forgotten records and finds that the ancestors of some people oppressed the ancestors of another, four hundred years ago; upon which he forthwith exhorts their descendants, living in peace and amity, to hate each other now. Another is more moderate: he only unearths the misgovernment of a hundred years ago as a present motive for mutual detestation." In this country, I should say, this last tendency prevails most with those who are not historians, but politicians. A more substantial drawback is the absorbing preoccupation of both the literary and the practical life; and the fact that there are only twenty-four hours in every day. Hamerton speaks of a Greek philosopher, who was suspected by the business men of incapacity for affairs, but who devoted a year to proving the contrary and traded with such skill that he went back to his studies a capitalist. The practical man is often benefited by being forced into study, and the student by taking, when it comes to him, his share in practical affairs; but no one supposes that their work, in the long run, can advantageously change hands.

XX

"MAKE THY OPTION WHICH OF TWO"

WHO does not look back with some slight envy to the period when Professor Popkin could dwell with longing on that coming day when he could retire from his Harvard Professorship of Greek and "read the authors"? He actually resigned in 1833, and had for nearly twenty years the felicity for which he longed. What he meant by reading the authors was well enough exhibited in that contemporary English clergyman, described in Hogg's "Life of Shelley," who devoted all his waking hours for thirty years to a regular course of Greek writers. He arranged them in a three years' course, and when they were ended he began again. The only exception was in case of Homer, whose works he read every year for a month at the seashore — "the proper place to read Homer," he said; and, as he also pointed out, there were twenty-four week-days in a

month, and by taking a book of the "Iliad"
before dinner, and a book of the "Odyssey"
after dinner, he just finished his pleasant task.
On rainy days, when he could not walk, he
threw in the Homeric hymns; he moreover
read a newspaper once a week, and occasionally
ran through a few pages of Virgil and Cicero,
just to satisfy himself that it was a waste of
time for any one who could read Greek to look
at anything else. Simple and perennial felicity! no vacillation, no variableness or shadow
of turning; no doubting between literature or
science, still less between this or that department of literature. Since all advisers bid us
read only the best books, why not follow their
counsel, and keep to Æschylus and Homer?

Who could have foreseen, in Dr. Popkin's day,
the vast expansion of modern literatures, which,
after exhausting all the Latin races, keeps opening upon us new treasure-houses elsewhere; so
that Mr. Howells would bid us all learn Russian
and Mr. Boyesen the Scandinavian tongues.
Who could have foreseen the relentless Max
Müller, marshalling before us by dozens the
Oriental religions; and Mr. Fitzgerald concen-

trating the wonders of them all into "Omàr Kháyyàm," who offers no religion whatever, and makes denial more eloquent than faith? Who had then dreamed of the Shakespearian literature, the Dantean literature, the Goethean literature; even the literature of Petrarch, as catalogued by Prof. Willard Fiske, to the extent of nearly a thousand entries? Who had looked forward to vast American historical works like Hubert Bancroft's fifty ample volumes on the Pacific Coast, or Winsor's "Narrative and Critical History of America"? Who had imagined the vast spread of magazine literature and of newspaper literature, threatening, as Mr. Holt the publisher predicts, to swamp all study of books beneath a vast deluge of serials and periodicals, to be traversed hereafter only with the aid of literary rafts, charts, and compasses? And then, when all this is enumerated, there is science, claiming itself to monopolize the intellectual world and sometimes intimating doubts whether the function of literature itself be not at an end.

In the very college where the peaceful Popkin once taught, there are now twenty-one distinct elective courses in Greek alone; and in all undergraduate branches not less than two hundred and thirty — each course offering occupation enough for a whole term's study, and some of them for that of a whole life. The "option which of two" described by Emerson as the painful necessity of later years, is here initiated in the earliest; and it is even proposed to carry it yet further into the preparatory schools by the alternative standards of admission. Even in Greek a single mood or tense of the verb is held to furnish material for a treatise; and so of every division and sub-division of all knowledge. Baron Osten Sacken, the entomologist, who during his stay in this country was our highest authority on the *Diptera*, or two-winged insects, always maintained that he had erred in marking out a range of study too vast for any single intellect; and that he should have done better to confine himself to some one family, as for instance, the *Culicidœ*, or gnats. There was nothing extreme in this confession; it might be paralleled in every department of study. But meanwhile what becomes of "the authors"?

I am not now speaking with any special

reference to the Greeks. The fate of the
ancient classics among us was long since settled.
When the successor of Dr. Popkin was made
President of Harvard College, in 1860, he
virtually surrendered his traditions by translating the Greek quotations in his Inaugural
Address ; and what President Felton did for the
elder language, President Eliot did for the
Latin when he, at the 250th anniversary of
that institution, bestowed the honorary degrees
in most sonorous English. Grant that the
" authors " now share with all other writers, in
all languages and departments, the limitations of
the life of man, it is plain that those limitations
bring the greatest change to those two languages
which were once thought to hold all knowledge
in their grasp. But the same stern restriction
makes itself felt in all directions; the age has
outgrown its few simple and convenient play-
things, and must choose amid a myriad of
edgetools.

There will never be another universal scholar.
The time when Aristotle or Plutarch went the
rounds of the universe, and tried to label each
phenomenon, looks now like the childhood of

the world, no matter how precocious the children. The period when Bacon sought to imitate them is scarcely nearer; and when that
great intellect found itself so overweighted with
the visible facts, it seems unkind for Mr.
Donnelly to burden him retrospectively with
even one cipher more. The omnivorous student, who would gladly keep the touch of all
branches of knowledge, finds them steadily
slipping away from him, and may be glad if he
can watch with fidelity the newest developments
in some single minute field, such as fossil cock-
roaches or the genitive case. It is useless for
Mr. Cabot to tell us that Emerson was not a
great scholar; we knew it already. He could
not in this age have been a great scholar and a
great writer. Thoreau resolutely limited himself to the observation of external nature in one
small township in Massachusetts; and he
assigned himself a task so far beyond his grasp
that we find him in his diaries puzzling over the
common brown cocoon of the *Attacus* moth as
if it was some wholly new phenomenon; indeed,
he seems scarcely to have noticed the insect
world at all. The best-trained observation, in

presence of the vast advance of knowledge, is very limited; and the human memory, instead of being, as people think, an india-rubber bag of indefinite expansion, is much more like those pop-guns made by boys, which are loaded with a bit of potato at one end, and another bit at the other, but never by any chance hold more than two bits of potato at the same time.

The acquisition of knowledge is, after all, a process of selection rather than of collection. We forget as fast as we learn, and it is doubtful if the most learned man really knows more at fifty than at twenty; he has merely driven out a multitude of insignificant details by those of greater value. The travelling salesman and the horse-car conductor are probably possessed of as many items of detached knowledge as Von Humboldt or Darwin; the difference is in their quality and their use. It was one of Margaret Fuller's acutest sayings that a man who expects to accomplish much in the world must learn after five and twenty to read with his fingers. Dr. Johnson, who said to the man who thanked God for his ignorance, "Then, sir, you have a great deal to be thankful for," was in a similar position to the person at whom he sneered, but was less frank in his ascriptions of gratitude. The elder Agassiz once said to me that so vast was becoming the multiplicity of publications in every branch of science, the time was approaching when no man would be able to write on any subject with the slightest sense of security. The hope is that by new intellectual facilities in the way of labor-saving methods, the human mind may become enabled to keep pace in some degree with this multiplying mass of studious materials, just as it keeps pace with vaster and vaster executive enterprises. It is pleasant to think, also, that the wider the range of fascinating knowledge, the stronger becomes the argument for continued personal identity. Next to the yearnings of human affection, the most irresistible suggestion of immortality comes from looking up at the unattainable mystery of the stars.

XXI

THE DECLINE OF THE SENTI-
MENTAL

AT a private charitable reading, held lately in Boston, it was noticed that the younger part of the audience responded but slightly in the way of sympathy to Dr. Holmes's poem on the Moore Festival, while to the older guests the allusions seemed all very familiar and even touching. The waning of sympathy for Moore and his "Irish Melodies" simply shows the diminished hold of the sentimental upon us, taking that word to represent a certain rather melodramatic self-consciousness, a tender intro-spection in the region of the heart, a kind of studious cosseting of one's finer feelings. Per-haps it is not generally recognized how much more abundant was this sort of thing forty years ago than now, and how it moulded the very temperaments of those who were born into it, and grew up under it. Byron had as much to do with creating it as any one in England; but more probably it goes back to Rousseau in France; hardly, I should think to Petrarch, to whom Lowell is disposed to attribute it, and who certainly exerted very little influence in the way of sentimentality on his friend Chaucer. But the Byronic atmosphere certainly spread to Germany, as may be seen by the place conceded to that poet in Goethe's "Faust;" although Goethe's "Werther," and Schiller's "Die Rauber" showed that the tendency itself was at one time indigenous everywhere. In England, Bulwer and the younger Disraeli aimed to be prose Byrons; and in Moore and Mrs. Hemans, followed by Mrs. Norton and "L. E. L.," we see the sentimental spirit in successive degrees of dilution.

All the vocal music of forty or fifty years ago — when the great German composers were but just beginning to make their power felt in this country — was of an intensely sentimental description; delightfully so, I might add, for those who were brought up to that kind of enjoyment. Moore's songs, such as "Believe Me if all those Endearing Young Charms," "Fly, fly from the World, O Bessy, with Me," "The

Harp that once through Tara's Halls," and a score of others, set the popular key-note; and even his hymns, such as " Come, Ye Disconsolate," had a similar flavor. The whole vocal literature of the day held the same pitch. Such songs as " Go Thou and dream," " Take hence the Bowl," " My Soul is Dark," " The Evening Gun," " Those Fairy Bells," were sung in every drawing-room, by a class of private singers more impassioned and more ardently dramatic than one now hears anywhere, and whose singing afforded a training in the emotional such as no experience of to-day can give. Their strength would now be considered a weakness; the exquisite German songs that now prevail, while far higher in musical quality, offer human feeling itself in a purer, simpler, and doubtless nobler form; but the die-away period had its own fascination — the period when even the military bands marched to the plaintive strains of Mrs. Norton's " Love Not."

In prose literature, as has been said, Bulwer and Disraeli best represented that epoch. The two fashionable novels, *par excellence*, of a whole generation, were " Pelham " and " Vivian

Grey." In the latter, all the heights of foppery and *persiflage* did but set off what was then regarded as the unsurpassable pathos of "Violet Fane's" death; and though the consummate dandyism of the companion book had no such relief, yet Bulwer amply made up for it by the rivers of tears that were shed over his "Pilgrims of the Rhine." Not a young lover of the period who had acquired a decent sentimental education, but was sure to put a flower between the leaves of that work where the author says: "Is there one of us who has not known a being for whom it would seem none too wild a fantasy, to indulge such a dream?" Yes, yes, Bulwer! interpreter of one's visions, everybody had known such an object of emotion; and a thousand plain Susans and Sarahs stood forever enshrined in that romantic creation — "the beautiful ideal of the world" — when death, or a luckier lover, or parental obduracy, or the mere accident of a family removal from New York to Cincinnati, had banished them from the regions of every day. Far be it from me to speak with disrespect of these emotions; it will presently be shown that they had many advantages; but in their full and unquestioned vigor they certainly belonged to the period when men wore cravats swathed half a dozen times round the neck, and when, as the author of " Pelham " wrote, there was safety in a swallow-tail.

It is not in the English tongue alone that this emotional tendency was expressed, for Lamartine was then much read, and even his travels in the East were saturated with it; and so were the writings of Jean Paul, who then rivalled Goethe in the affections of the newly enrolled students of German. His " Siebenkäs " which avowedly records the " life, death, and wedding " of a hero who deliberately counterfeits death, that he and his mismated wife may each espouse the object of a loftier tenderness, was the climax of the sentimental; and yet this preposterous situation was so seriously and sympathetically painted, that probably no one who read the book at that day can now revert to it without emotion. But it is necessary to bear all this in mind in order to understand how all this atmosphere of exaggerated feeling seemed blown away in an instant by the first appearance of Sam Weller on the scene.

Dickens himself bore marked traces of the very epidemic he banished, and his Little Nells and Little Pauls were the last survival of the sentimental period ; but nevertheless, it was he, more than any one else, who exorcised it; and whatever its merits, he rendered the world a service in that act of grace.

Yet no one can really regret, I should say, to have been born during that earlier period; it suffused life with a certain charm; and though it may sometimes have prematurely exhausted the heart, it oftener kept it young. For as we grow older we revert to the associations of our youth; what prevailed then seems always desirable; if our youth was a period of compression, our age is doubly such, but if that early period had emotional freedom and *epanchement*, our old age will have the same. Those who were in the current of the transcendental movement that swept through Europe and America half a century ago, will probably always have a touch of sentimentalism in their sympathies, a little exuberance somewhere, even when the outside is hard or constrained; and even those who belong to a later school may show traces of that which prevailed when they were in their cradles, as Howells's volume of poems opens with the sentimental and even beautiful strains of " Forlorn." This, then, was the path through which he came to Silas Lapham and Lemuel Barker; and very likely, when Mr. Henry James's biography comes to be written, he may yet be found to have begun by taking tremulous footsteps in some such romantic path. After all, sentimentalism is a thing immortal, for it represents the slight overplus and excess of youthful emotion ; it bears the same relation to the deeper feelings of later life that the college contests of the football ground bear to life's conflicts. Tennyson, who began by representing it, and then, with a hand far finer than that of Dickens, helped to guide us out of it, has unconsciously described the service done to the age by the epoch of sentimentalism when he paints in his " Gardener's Daughter," the mission fulfilled by Juliet, the earliest object of his flame : —

> " The summer pilot of an empty heart
> Unto the shores of nothing. Know you not
> Such touches are but embassies of love
> To tamper with the feelings, ere he found
> Empire for life ? "

XXII

CONCERNING GIANTS

NOTHING shows the way in which fame concentrates itself on certain leading figures more effectually than an inspection of book catalogues. For instance, the British Museum catalogue gives fifty-eight folio pages — with double columns and small type — to its Dante entries. The forthcoming catalogue of the Dante collection in the Harvard College Library will include about eleven hundred titles; this being just about the size of the great collection of "Petrarch Books" lately catalogued by its owner, Prof. Willard Fiske, formerly of Cornell University. The whole body of Dantean literature, it is estimated by experts, must extend to between two and three thousand titles; and the Napoleonic literature has been estimated, or rather guessed, at five thousand. The Barton Shakespearean collection in the Boston Public Library includes about a thousand titles under the "works" of Shakespeare, and fifteen hundred more under "Shakespeareana." It is certain that all these special collections are very incomplete, and it is altogether probable that all these estimates are too scanty. If they are not, they soon will be, since all these special literatures are increasing all the time. More than a hundred titles have been added to the Dante list, for instance, during the past year; and the Petrarch quinquecentennial called forth one hundred and twenty-five new works about that poet in Italy alone. If anything is certain, it is that, when the world has once definitely accepted a man as among the elect, his fame and his lead over his contemporaries go on increasing with the passing years. It is possible that the *Académie Française* may yet be chiefly remembered because it rejected Molière, as the mighty Persian conqueror had a place in fame simply as one who knew not the worth of Firdousi.

"Literature," it has been said, is "attar of roses: one distilled drop from a million petals." Those who learned their Italian nearly half a century ago will remember that the favorite text-book was named, "The Four Poets" (*I Quattro Poeti*). But Ariosto and Tasso are now practically dropped out of the running; and those who still read Petrarch are expected to treat rather deferentially those for whom Italian literature means Dante only. Yet Voltaire wrote of Dante, only a century and a half ago, that although occasionally, under favorable circumstances, he wrote lines not unworthy of Tasso or Ariosto, yet his work was, as a whole, "stupidly extravagant and barbarous." "The Italians," he says, "call him divine, but it is a hidden divinity; few people understand his oracles. He has commentators, which is perhaps another reason for his not being understood. His reputation will go on increasing, because scarce anybody reads him." How little he was known in England a hundred years ago may be seen from the fact that Dr. Nathan Drake, who had quite a name as a critic a century ago, spoke of Dr. Darwin's placid and pedantic poem, "The Botanic Garden," as showing "the wild and terrible sublimity of Dante." A hundred years from this have ended in Ruskin's characterization of Dante as "the

central man of all the world, as representing in
perfect balance the imaginative, moral, and
intellectual faculties, all at their highest."
When we consider that this was said of a man
born more than six centuries before the words
were written, it certainly illustrates the concentration of fame upon a single name. With
scarcely less superb exclusiveness, Goethe
described Napoleon as "a compendium of the
world" (*Dieses Compendium der Welt*).

In allusion to such instances as these, Goethe
expressed to Eckermann the conviction that the
higher powers had pleased themselves by placing among men certain detached figures, so
alluring as to set everybody striving after
them, yet so great as to be beyond all reach
(*Die so anlockend sind, das jeder nach ihnen
strebt, und so gross das niemand sie erreicht*).
"Mozart," he said, "represents the unattainable in music, and Shakespeare in poetry."
He instanced also Raphael and Napoleon; and
the loyal Eckermann inwardly added the
speaker himself to the list. "I refer" Goethe
said "to the natural dowry, the inborn wealth"
(*Das Naturell, das grosse Angeborene der*

Natur). It will be a theme for never-ending discussion how far this concentration is really due to the exceptional greatness of the subject, and how far to the tendency of genius to draw to itself all the floating materials of the time, to drain its best intellects, to reflect its best impulses. Dante, of all great writers, is the least explainable in this way; but in the case of Shakespeare, of Voltaire, of Goethe, it is obvious enough. The last named was always ready to admit his own obligations, not merely to his own fellow-countrymen, as Schiller, but to Englishmen and Frenchmen; and was profoundly moved on receiving the first French version of his "Faust," from the thought of the profound influence exercised by Voltaire and his great contemporaries over him as over the whole civilized world. Humbler men are constantly obliged to recognize how they themselves have been fed and nourished by those lowlier still; and we may be very sure that the greatest are formed in the same way, and draw from many obscure and even inexplicable sources, as Heine claims that he learned all the history of the French Revolution through the drumming of an old French drummer.

It is obvious enough that the relative proportions of printed matter do not precisely reflect
absolute merit, because they are liable to be
influenced by trivial considerations, apart from
personal qualities. The Man in the Iron Mask
was not necessarily a great man because he
occasioned an extensive literature; and Junius
fills the library as an inexhaustible conundrum,
whereas plain Sir Philip Francis might never
have elicited even a biography. Had Shelley
been the contented husband of one wife, or had
Poe selected any one city to dwell in and dwelt
there, it is certain that the Shelley literature
and the Poe literature would have been far
slenderer in dimensions, though the genius of
the poets might have remained the same. It is
the personal qualities, in such cases, that multi-
ply the publications, though it is quite true, on
the other side, that Poe might have lived un-
noticed in more cities than claimed Homer had
it not been for "The Raven," and that Shelley
might have had as many wives as a Mormon
but for "The Skylark." As time goes on, it is
the thought of the poet more than the gossip
about his life which holds and creates literature,

and there are always a dozen who wish to unlock the mystery of Hamlet for one who demands positive evidence as to Shakespeare's wedded bliss. But, however we explain it, there is such a tendency of study and criticism toward concentration on single figures, that no nation in the course of centuries can furnish more than two or three; and it is much for any people if it can furnish one. The growing proportions of the Emerson literature leave little doubt who is to provide for America — if, indeed, any one is to supply it — that central and controlling figure.

XXIII

WEAPONS OF PRECISION

WHEN in July, 1609, the Iroquois Indians first saw a gun fired, and saw two men fall dead at a distance, because the Sieur de Champlain had raised something to his cheek, they were so utterly frightened that the whole tribe ran away, abandoning their camp and their provisions. Yet the gun was only a short weapon, then called an arquebus, and loaded with four balls. It did not take long for these very Indians to learn the use of the arquebus; and yet, if one of them were to come to life again and look at a modern rifle, it would cause him as much amazement as if he had never seen a firearm. These delicate grooves and spiral curves would strike him as a piece of mere affectation; and he would prefer by all means an honest old-fashioned affair that would send a bullet straight to its mark. He would not be convinced until he again saw a man fall dead, and this time at an incredible distance, by an invisible blow.

Now, style in writing is a weapon far more delicate and more formidable than the latest form of needle-gun. It will not merely kill a man's body at the range of a thousand yards, but his reputation at a distance of centuries. Nay, it will not only kill, but it will keep alive, which may be worse; keep the stained memory in existence beyond the possibility of a happy oblivion —and so also with memories of good. So long as it remains crude and undeveloped, language has not acquired this capability; but every added refinement of touch, every improved note of precision, will expand and perfect this carrying power. The blunt repartee of the mining-camp may furnish as good a prelude as any other for drawing a revolver from the hip pocket; but the effect of the saying dies with the duel and the funeral. It takes the fine rapier of Talleyrand's wit to impale an opponent for a hundred years upon a single delicate phrase, intervening between the smile and the snuff-box.

The French language has doubtless a peculiar capacity in this direction, sharpened by the steady practice of generations; but the English

language comes next to it, could we only out-
grow the impression that there is no honesty in
anything but a knock-down blow, and that all
finer touches are significant of sin; that boxing
is a manly exercise, in short, while fencing is
not. It is a curious fact, however, that as the
best American manners incline to the French
and not the English model, so the tendency of
American literary style is to the finer methods,
quicker repartees, and more delicate turns.
People complain, and with some justice, of a certain thinness in the material of Mr. Howells's
conversations; but his phrases are not so thin
as the edge of a Damascus blade, and where the
life itself is to be reached, this keenness has a
certain advantage. We are constantly told by
English critics that in real life people do not
talk in this way, to which the answer is, that
the scene of his novels is not laid in England.

Lightness of touch is the final test of power.
*Où il n'y a point de délicatesse, il n'y a point de
littérature.* Joubert goes on to add that where
there is shown in literary style only the attribute of strength, the style expresses character
alone, not training. There has come lately a

certain slovenliness into the vocabulary of
Englishmen which is a sign of weakness, not
of strength. It may be meant for strength,
but, like swearing, it is rather a substitute for
it. When Matthew Arnold, at the outset of
his paper on Emerson, proposes that we should
"pull ourselves together" to examine him, he
says crudely what might have been more forci-
bly conveyed by a finer touch. When Mr.
Gosse, in one of his *Forum* papers, answers an
objection with "A fiddlestick's end for such a
theory!" it does not give an impression of
vigor, or of what he calls, in case of Dryden,
"a virile tramp," but rather suggests that
humbler hero of whom Byron records that —

"He knew not what to say, and so he swore."

The fact that Mr. Arnold and Mr. Gosse have
both made good criticisms on others does not
necessarily indicate that they practise as they
preach. To come back once more to the incom-
parable Joubert, we often find a good ear perfectly compatible with a false note. *Que de
gens, en littérature, ont l'oreille juste, et chantent
faux!*

It is never worth while to dwell much upon
international comparisons; it is enough to say
that the oft-criticised want of the art-instinct in
English-speaking nations shows itself, though
in a less degree, in literature also, and renders
constant watchfulness needful lest we revert
into brutality. In this respect modern Germany can teach us little, save through the
Franco-German Heine. A young American
usually comes home from a German university
with more knowledge than when he went
there, but with less power of felicitous expression. But Greece and Rome have still unex-
hausted lessons, and so have Persia and Arabia;
these last, indeed, wreathe their weapons with
too many roses, but they carry true nevertheless. Dante not only created his own concep-
tions, but almost the very language in which
he wrote; and what was his power of expression we can judge best by seeing in how few
lines he can put vividly before us some theme
which Tennyson or Browning afterward ham-
mers out into a long poem. In English literature there seemed to be developing, in the time
of Addison, something of that steady, even,

felicitous power which makes French prose so remarkable; but it has passed, since his day, possibly from excess of vigor, into a prolonged series of experiments. Johnson experimentalized in one direction, Coleridge in another; Landor, Macaulay, Carlyle, Ruskin, in other directions still; and the net result is an uncertain type of style, which has almost always vigor and sometimes beauty, but is liable at any moment to relapse into Rider Haggard and "a fiddlestick's end." It is hard for our modest American speech to hold its own, now that the potent influence of Emerson has passed away; but we are lost unless we keep resolutely in mind that prose style ought not to be merely a bludgeon or a boomerang, but should be a weapon of precision.

XXIV

THE TEST OF THE DIME NOVEL

NO work of fiction ever published in London, the newspapers say, received so many advance orders as greeted a late story by Mr. Haggard. It is a curious illustration of the difference between the current literary tendencies of England and America, that in the mother-country alone are authors of this type taken seriously. The sale of their works is often larger here than in England, for the same reason which makes the combined circulation of daily newspapers so much larger; but they are no more considered as forming a part of literature than one would include in a "History of the Drama" some sworn statement as to the number of tickets sold for a Christmas pantomime. When a certain Mr. Mansfield Tracy Walworth was murdered near New York, a few years ago, it came out incidentally that he had written a novel called "Warwick," of which seventy-five thousand copies had been sold, and another called "Delaplaine," that had gone up to forty-five thousand. Another author of the same school, known as "Ned Buntline," is said to have earned sixty thousand dollars in a single year by his efforts; and still another, Sylvanus Cobb, Jr., is known to have habitually received a salary of ten thousand dollars for publications equally popular. No community can do without such books, but in America they are not usually counted as literature. Their authors scarcely obtain even the cheap immortality of the encyclopædia. Such books are innocent enough; they are simply harmless weeds that grow up wherever the soil is rich, and sometimes where it is barren; science must catalogue them impartially, but they are not reckoned as a part of the horticultural product. The peculiarity is, that in England Mr. Haggard's crop of weeds is counted into the harvest; his preposterous plots are gravely discussed, compared, and criticised; he is himself admitted into the *Contemporary Review* as a valued contributor; Mr. Lang writes books with him; his success lies not merely in his publisher's balance, like that of Mr. Walworth, Mr. Cobb, or "Ned Buntline," but it is a *succès d'estime*.

When, on the other hand, one opens an American daily paper to see what is said about the latest Haggard publication, one is likely to happen upon something like this: "We grudge it the few necessary lines . . . The illustrations are worthy of what they illustrate, and a second-rate imagination runs riot in pictures and text." Even this, perhaps, is giving too much space to the matter; but even if a London critic wished to say just this, he would say it on such a scale as if he were discussing a posthumous work by George Eliot. This difference is the more to be noticed because there was surely a time when the externals of good writing, at least, were held in high esteem at London; and the critics of that metropolis were wont to give but short shrift to any book which disregarded those conditions. But that which practically excludes Mr. Haggard from the ranks of serious and accredited writers is not that his sentiment is melodramatic, his fancy vulgar, and his situations absurd; the more elementary ground of exclusion is that he

makes fritters of English. It is hard for criticism to deal seriously with a novelist who
writes: "It is us;" "He . . . read on like
some one reads in some ghastly dream;"
"Jacobus . . . whom was exceedingly sick;"
"So that was where they were being taken to;"
and the like. In the *Contemporary Review*
his style seems to have been revised editori-
ally, and we find nothing worse than such
slang phrases as "played out," though this is
certainly bad enough. If a man in decent
society should place his feet upon the table
but once, his standing would be as effectually
determined as if his offences had been seventy
times seven.

Now, whatever may be said of current
tendencies in American literature, it may at
least be claimed that our leading novelists do
not tilt back their chairs or put their feet upon
the table. Mr. Howells, for instance, has his
defects, and may be proceeding, just now, upon
a theory too narrow; but it is impossible to
deny that he recognizes the minor morals of
literary art. His sentences hold well together;
he does not gush, does not straggle, gives no

passages of mere twaddle. He does not, like William Black, catch the same salmon over again so many times in a single story, and with such ever-increasing fulness of detail, that Izaak Walton himself would at last be bored into an impulse of forbearance; he does not, like Clark Russell, keep his heroine for nearly a year running about half-clothed over scorching rocks upon a tropical island, and then go into raptures over the dazzling whiteness of her bosom. So in the use of language, Howells does not, like Hardy, write "tactical observation" where he means "tactful;" or, like Haggard, say "those sort of reflections." It is a curious thing that on the very points where America formerly went to school to England, we should now have to praise our own authors for setting a decent example.

Can it be that, as time goes on, the habit of careful writing is one day to be set aside carelessly, as a mere American whim? In Professor Bain's essay "On Teaching English, with Detailed Examples" one finds such phrases on the part of the author as "Sixty themes *or thereby* are handled in these pages" (p. 38), and "The whole of the instruction in higher English might be *overtaken* in such a course" (p. 48); the italics being my own. If such are the "detailed examples" given by professional teachers in England, what is to become of the followers? It is encouraging, perhaps, to see that the prolonged American resistance to the Anglicism "different to" may be having a little reflex influence, when the *Spectator* describes Tennyson's second "Locksley Hall" as being "different from" his first. The influence is less favorable when we find one of the most local and illiterate of American colloquialisms reappearing in the *Pall Mall Gazette*, where it says: "Even Mr. Sala is better known, *we expect*, for his half-dozen books," etc. But the most repellent things one sees in English books, in the way of language, are the coarsenesses for which no American is responsible, as when in the graceful writings of Juliana Ewing the reader comes upon the words "stinking" or "nigger." This last offensive word is also invariably used by Froude in "Oceana." Granting that taste and decorum are less important than logic and precision, it seems as if even these last qualities must have become a little impaired when we read in the *Saturday Review* such curious lapses as this: "At home we have only the infinitely little, the speeches of infinitesimal members of Parliament. . . . In America matters yet more minute occupy the press." More minute than the infinitely little and the infinitesimal!

It will be a matter of deep regret to all thoughtful Americans should there ever be a distinct lowering of the standard of literary workmanship in England. The different branches of the English-speaking race are mutually dependent; they read each other's books; they need to co-operate in keeping up the common standard. It is too much to ask of any single nation that it should do this alone. Can it be that the real source of the change, if it is actually in progress, may be social rather than literary? It is conceivable that the higher status of the dime novel in England may be simply a part of that reversion toward a lower standard which grows naturally out of an essentially artificial social structure. Is it possible that some strange and abnormal results should not follow where one man is raised to the peerage because he is a successful brewer, and another because he is Alfred Tennyson? No dozen poets or statesmen, it is said, would have been so mourned in England as was Archer the jockey; nor did Holmes or Lowell have a London success so overpowering as that of "Buffalo Bill." In a community which thus selects its heroes, why should not the highest of all wreaths of triumph be given to Mr. Haggard's Umslopagaas, "that dreadful-looking, splendid savage"?

XXV

THE TRICK OF SELF-DEPRECIATION

THE two great branches of the English-speaking race have this in common, that they criticise themselves very frankly, in a way one rarely finds among Germans or Frenchmen. It comes, perhaps, from the habit of local self-government. If the streets are not well lighted, or if one's horse stumbles over an ill-kept pavement, the natural impulse is to complain of it to every one we meet, and to write about it in the local newspaper. Instead of putting only our strong points forward, we are always ready to discuss our weakest side. This must always be remembered in digesting the criticisms of Englishmen. Dickens, Carlyle, Ruskin, Arnold, have said nothing about Americans more unpleasant than they had previously said about their own countrymen; and why should we expect to fare any better? It is only in foreign countries that even we Americans stand up

resolutely for our own land. I lived for some
time with a returned fellow-countryman of very
keen wit, who, after long residence in Europe,
found nothing to please him at home. One
day, meeting one of his European companions,
I was asked, "How is ——? Does he stand up
for everything American, through thick and
thin, as he used to do in Florence?" Turning upon my neighbor with this unexpected
supply of ammunition, I was met with the
utmost frankness. He owned that while in
Europe he had defended all American ways,
through loyalty, and that he criticised them at
home for the same reason. "I shall abuse my
own country," he said, "so long as I think it
is worth saving. When that hope is gone, I
shall praise it."

In the once famous poem of "Festus," recalled lately to memory by its fiftieth anniversary, there is a fine passage about the useless-
ness of indiscriminate censure : —

> "The worst way to improve the world
> Is to condemn it. Men may overget
> Delusion, not despair."

For example, I cannot help admiring the patient

fidelity with which my old friend Professor
Norton holds up everything among us to an
ideal standard, and censures what he thinks
the vanity of our nation. But those who
think with me that behind that apparent vanity
there is a real self-distrust, which is a greater
evil, — those who think that timidity, not con-
ceit, is our real national foible, — can easily see
how these very criticisms foster that timidity;
so that " meek young men grow up in libraries,"
in Emerson's phrase, who feel that what they
can say can claim no weight in either continent, so long as they do not say it in the *Saturday Review*. So some rather impulsive remarks
in a New York newspaper as to the large
number of persons in this country, as in all
countries, who assume a clean shirt but once
a week, probably did little or no good to the
offending individuals, while it has winged a
fatal arrow for Matthew Arnold's bow, as for
many others. Comparisons are often mislead-
ing. David Urquhart, the English traveller,
was always denouncing his fellow-countrymen
as exceedingly dirty when compared with the
Mohammedan races, and used to wish that

Charles Martel had not finally driven back the Saracen forces at the battle of Tours, because if he had been defeated, Urquhart says, the Mohammedans would have overrun all Europe, " and then even we English should have been gentlemen."

Of all the points on which we Americans are apt to satirize ourselves, the much-discussed American girl is the most available. There is not in this wide land a journalist so callow as not to be able, when news runs short, to turn a paragraph on this theme, with some epigram as sparkling as his brains and as comprehensive as his experience. Thus, opening a Western magazine, one comes upon the amazing statement that the New York girl " dines heavily, drinks wine at all meals, smokes cigarettes, and revels at all times in the effects of the most advanced usages," — whatever this last vague and awful intimation may mean. On the next page the same author assures us, with equally close and unerring knowledge, that "the Southern girl is the most truly learned of her sex; . . . she is seldom otherwise than beautiful; . . . she plays all classical music without notes." Why are we so severe on poor stray Englishmen, who know no better, when we ourselves furnish such social observation as this? Yet this kind of thing may be read far and wide under the head of "Society Chit-chat," and is apt to leave the impression that the writer was about as near to the wondrous creatures he describes as that coachman mentioned by Horace Walpole, who, having driven certain maids of honor for many years, left his savings to his son on condition that this chosen heir should never marry a maid of honor.

The real test of the manners and morals of a nation is not by comparison with other nations, but with itself. It must be judged by the historical, not by the topographical, standard. Does it develop? and how? Manners, like morals, are an affair of evolution, and must often be a native product, — a wholly indigenous thing. This is the case, for instance, with the habitual American courtesy to women in travelling, — a thing unparalleled in any European country, and of which, even in this country, Howells finds his best type in the Cali-

fornian. What comes nearest to it among the
Latin races is the courtesy of the high-bred
gentleman toward the lady who is his social
equal, which is a wholly different thing. A
similar point of evolution in this country is the
decorum of a public assembly. It is known
that at the early town meetings in New England men sat with their hats on, as in England.
Unconsciously, by a simple evolution of good
manners, the practice has been outgrown in
America; but Parliament still retains it. Many
good results may have followed imperceptibly
from this same habit of decorum. Thus Mr.
Bryce points out that the forcible interruption
of a public meeting by the opposite party,
although very common in England, is very rare
in America. In general, with us, usages are
more flexible, more adaptive; in public meetings, for instance, we get rid of a great many
things that are unutterably tedious, as the
English practice of moving, seconding, and
debating the prescribed vote of thanks to the
presiding officer at the end of the most insignificant gathering. It is very likely that even

our incessant self-criticism contributes toward this gradual amelioration of habits. In that case the wonder is, that our English cousins, who criticise themselves quite as incessantly, should move so slowly.

XXVI

THE LITERARY PENDULUM

AFTER all," said the great advocate Rufus Choate, "a book is the only immortality." That was the lawyer's point of view; but the author knows that, even after the book is published, the immortality is often still to seek. In the depressed moods of the advocate or the statesman, he is apt to imagine himself as writing a book; and when this is done, it is easy enough to carry the imagination a step farther and to make the work a magnificent success; just as, if you choose to fancy yourself a foreigner, it is as easy to be a duke as a tinker. But the professional author is more often like Christopher Sly, whose dukedom is in dreams; and he is fortunate if he does not say of his own career with Christopher: " A very excellent piece of work, good madam lady. Would 'twere done ! "

In our college days we are told that men change, while books remain unchanged. But in

a very few years we find that the circle of books
alters as swiftly and strangely as that of the
men who write or the boys who read them.
When the late Dr. Walter Channing of Boston
was revisiting in old age his birthplace, Newport, R.I., he requested me to take him to the
Redwood Library, of which he had been librarian some sixty years before. He presently
asked the librarian, with an eagerness at first
inexplicable, for a certain book, whose name I
had never before heard. With some difficulty
the custodian hunted it up, entombed beneath
other dingy folios in a dusty cupboard. Nobody,
he said, had ever before asked for it during his administration. "Strange!" said Dr. Channing,
turning over the leaves. "This was in my time
the show-book of the collection; people came
here purposely to see it." He closed it with a
sigh, and it was replaced in its crypt. Dr.
Channing is dead, the librarian who unearthed
the book is since dead, and I have forgotten its
very title. In all coming time, probably, its
repose will be as undisturbed as that of Hans
Andersen's forgotten Christmas-tree in the gar-
ret. Did, then, the authorship of that book give

to its author so very substantial a hold on immortality ?

But there is in literary fame such a thing as recurrence — a swing of the pendulum which at first brings despair to the young author, yet yields him at last his only consolation. *L'éternité est une pendule,* wrote Jacques Bridaine, that else forgotten Frenchman whose phrase gave Longfellow the hint of his "Old Clock on the Stair." When our professors informed us that books remained unchanged, those of us who were studious at once pinched ourselves to buy books ; but the authors for whom we made economies in our wardrobe are now as obsolete, very likely, as the garments that we exchanged for them. No undergraduate would now take off my hands at half price, probably, the sets of Landor's "Imaginary Conversations" and Coleridge's "Literary Remains," which it once seemed worth a month of threadbare elbows to possess. I lately called the attention of a young philologist to a tolerably full set of Thomas Taylor's translations, and found that he had never heard of even the name of that servant of obscure learning. In college we studied

Cousin and Jouffroy, and he who remembers the rise and fall of all that ambitious school of French eclectics can hardly be sure of the permanence of Herbert Spencer, the first man since their day who has undertaken to explain the whole universe of being. How we used to read Hazlitt, whose very name is so forgotten that an accomplished author has lately duplicated the title of his most remarkable book, "Liber Amoris," without knowing that it had ever been used! What a charm Irving threw about the literary career of Roscoe; but who now recognizes his name? Ardent youths, eager to combine intellectual and worldly success, fed themselves in those days on "Pelham" and "Vivian Grey;" but these works are not now even included in "Courses of Reading" — that last infirmity of noble fames. One may look in vain through the vast mausoleum of Bartlett's "Dictionary of Quotations" for even that one maxim of costume, which was "Pelham's" bid for immortality.

Literary fame is, then, by no means a fixed increment, but a series of vibrations of the pendulum. Happy is that author who comes to be

benefited by an actual return of reputation —
as athletes get beyond the period of breathless-
ness, and come to their "second wind." Yet
this is constantly happening. Emerson, visiting Landor in 1847, wrote in his diary, "He
pestered me with Southey — but who is
Southey?" Now, Southey had tasted fame
more promptly than his greater contemporaries,
and liked the taste so well that he held his
own poems far superior to those of Wordsworth, and wrote of them, "With Virgil, with
Tasso, with Homer, there are fair grounds of
comparison." Then followed a period during
which the long shades of oblivion seemed to
have closed over the author of "Madoc" and
"Kehama." Behold! in 1886 the *Pall Mall
Gazette*, revising through "the best critics"
Sir James Lubbock's "Hundred Best Books,"
dethrones Byron, Shelley, Coleridge, Lamb, and
Landor; omits them all, and reinstates the forgotten Southey once more. Is this the final
award of fate? No: it is simply the inevitable
swing of the pendulum.

Southey, it would seem, is to have two
innings; perhaps one day it will yet be Hayley's

turn. "Would it please you very much," asks
Warrington of Pendennis, "to have been the
author of Hayley's verses?" Yet Hayley was,
in his day, as Southey testifies, "by popular
election the king of the English poets;" and he
was held so important a personage that he received, what probably no other author ever has
won, a large income for the last twelve years of
his life in return for the prospective copyright
of his posthumous memoirs. Miss Anna Seward,
writing in 1786, ranks him, with the equally
forgotten Mason, as "the two foremost poets
of the day;" she calls Hayley's poems "mag-
nolias, roses, and amaranths," and pronounces
his esteem a distinction greater than monarchs
hold it in their power to bestow. But probably nine out of ten who shall read these lines
will have to consult a biographical dictionary to
find out who Hayley was; while his odd *protégé*,
William Blake, whom the fine ladies of the day
wondered at Hayley for patronizing, is now the
favorite of literature and art.

So strong has been the recent swing of the
pendulum in favor of what is called realism in
fiction, it is very possible that if Hawthorne's

" Twice-told Tales " were to appear for the first
time to-morrow they would attract no more
attention than they did fifty years ago. Mr.
Stockton has lately made a similar suggestion
as to the stories of Edgar Poe. Perhaps this
gives half a century as the approximate measure of the variations of fate — the periodicity
of the pendulum. On the other hand, Jane
Austen, who would, fifty years ago, have been
regarded as an author suited to desolate islands
or long and tedious illnesses, has now come to
be the founder of a school, and must look
down benignly from heaven to see the brightest
minds assiduously at work upon that " little bit
of ivory, two inches square " by which she symbo-
lized her novels. Then comes in, as an alternative, the strong Russian tribe, claimed by realists as real, by idealists as ideal, and perhaps
forcing the pendulum in a new direction.
Nothing, surely, since Hawthorne's death, has
given us so much of the distinctive flavor of
his genius as Tourguenéff's extraordinary
" Poems in Prose " in the admirable version of
Mrs. T. S. Perry.

But the question, after all, recurs : why

should we thus be slaves of the pendulum? Why should we not look at these vast variations of taste more widely, and, as it were, astronomically, to borrow Thoreau's phrase? In the mind of a healthy child there is no incongruity between fairy tales and the Rollo Books; and he passes without disquiet from the fancied heart-break of a tin soldier to Jonas mending an old rat-trap in the barn. Perhaps, after all, the literary fluctuation occurs equally in their case and in ours, but under different conditions. It may be that, in the greater mobility of the child's nature, the pendulum can swing to and fro in half a second of time and without the consciousness of effort; while in the case of older readers, the same vibration takes half a century of time and the angry debate of a thousand journals.

XXVII

THE EVOLUTION OF AN AMERICAN

EMERSON once wrote, "We go to Europe to be Americanized." In the recent *Correspondence of John Lothrop Motley* — the most attractive series of letters which the present writer has for many a day encountered — the most interesting feature, after all, is the gradual evolution of an American. Wendell Phillips used to delight in testifying to the manner in which this process went on in this his classmate and friend, and also in himself. Both came out of Harvard College, Phillips said, the narrow aristocrats of a petty sphere; both — though he did not say this — handsome, elegant, accomplished, the prime favorites of the small but really polished circle of the Boston of that day. In case of Phillips, the emancipation was more rapid; and he too owed it in a sense to Europe, for it was there he met his future wife, through whom he first became interested in the anti-slavery movement. In Motley's case the change came more slowly, and reached its crisis at the outbreak of the Civil War; and it must have been at the time of his arrival in this country in 1861 that he met Phillips with the ardent exclamation, as the latter used to repeat it, "Phillips, you were right, and I was wrong!" This may, however, have been when he visited home in 1858, for his dissatisfaction with the pro-slavery tendency of public affairs was manifest as early as 1855.[1]

I can remember well my first impression of Motley and his friend and afterward brother-in-law, Stackpole, as the acknowledged leaders of the Boston society of which I had an occasional boyish glimpse; and the glamour of youth still remains strong enough to make it impossible for me to believe that any drawing-room was ever ruled by more elegant and distinguished men. There was a younger brother — nearer my own age — Preble Motley, who was an athlete as well as an Antinous, and hence doubly the idol of his compeers; and his early death was caused, in the traditions of that time, by a too daring excess in those gymnastic exercises which were

---

[1] Correspondence, i. 170, 268.

just beginning to come into vogue. The elder
brother was of a more delicate and poetic
mould; and it could be said of him, as is said
of the prophet Mohammed in the Sheeah traditions, that " his manners charmed all mankind."
Hence he found himself readily at home in the
court society of Vienna, to which he was first
sent; and when he was transferred to England,
he felt keenly the delight at finding, with a
shade less of elegance in the society around him,
a recognition which he had not before encountered, of purely intellectual claims. Hence we
find him in the first volume of his letters lavish-
ing praises on London society, such as he was
by no means ready to reaffirm after the crucial
test of our Civil War had been applied.   In the
earlier days, too, he naturally contrasted the
accumulated intellectual wealth of Europe with·
the comparative poverty of his own land in
these respects. "When I see here in Europe
such sums of money spent by the government
upon every branch of the fine arts, I cannot help
asking why we at home have no picture-galleries,
or statue-galleries, or libraries. I cannot see at
all that such things are only fit for monarchies." [1]

[1] Correspondence i. 29.

This was in his student days in 1833; and it would now seem less appropriate were it not that our barbarous tariff on works of art is still continued; and a later complaint, in 1851, that our American rivers are "deaf and dumb" for want of literary associations [1] is rapidly growing obsolete.

The habitual and still lingering indifference of Europeans to all matters in the New World had already struck Motley in 1852, at the time of Daniel Webster's death, when he found scarcely any one on the European continent who had ever heard his name, although one literary lady had an impression that he was one of our principal poets. Nobody in England supposed that he was in any way to be ranked with their public men — such as Lord Brougham, for instance. "The fact is," he adds, "no interest is felt in America or American institutions among the European public. America is as isolated as China. Nobody knows or cares anything about its men, or its politics, or its conditions. It is, however, known and felt among the lower classes that it is a place to get to out

[1] Correspondence, i. 125.

of the monotonous prison-house of Philistines, in which the great unwashed of Europe continue to grind eternally. Very little is known of the country, and very little respect is felt for it; but the fact remains that Europe is decanting itself into America a great deal more rapidly than is to be wished by us." [1]

While trying to work away on his history Motley found himself absorbed not only in our great conflict, which made European politics seem "pale and uninteresting," but in the extraordinary way in which it set at naught all European traditions. "All European ideas are turned upside down by the mere statement of the proposition, which is at the bottom of our war. Hitherto 'the sovereignty of the people' has been heard in Europe, and smiled at as a fiction. . . . But now here comes rebellion against our idea of sovereignty, and fact on a large scale is illustrating our theoretic fiction." [2] In the next letter he uses that fine phrase which illustrates so much in our early struggles and difficulties through that contest: "It is not a military war, if such a contradiction can be

<hr>

[1] Correspondence, i. 147.   [2] Ibid., ii. 79.

used. It is a great political and moral revolution, and we are in the first stage of it." [1] This
was the period of which the English Hayward
wrote, — the translator of "Faust," — "I passed
a day with the Motleys at their villa, and found
him more unreasonable than ever, vowing that
the restoration of the Union in its entirety was
as sure as the sun in heaven." It was the
period of which Motley himself afterward wrote,
"All English 'society,' except half a dozen
individuals, was then entirely Southern."

It was, in short, the opening of that period of
cleavage between the English and American
literary classes which still bears its fruit in the
habits of mind of this generation, and will
never be forgotten till a new generation has
wholly taken its place. The fact that the
literary class especially, which in other countries is usually found on the side of progress,
in this case echoed all the sympathies of the
people of rank, and left only the workingmen
of England, with a few illustrious exceptions,
to be our friends — this it was that made Motley
not merely a patriot, but a man of democratic

1 Correspondence, ii. 82.

convictions at last. In 1862 he wrote, "I am so much of a democrat; far more than I ever was before in my life." [1] Two years later he writes, — this man of experience in many courts, — "For one, I like democracy. I don't say that it is pretty, or genteel, or jolly. But it has a reason for existing, and is a fact in America, and is founded on the immutable principles of reason and justice. Aristocracy certainly presents more brilliant social phenomena, more luxurious social enjoyments. Such a system is very cheerful for a few thousand select specimens out of the few hundred millions of the human race . . . but what a price is paid for it!" [2] When he wrote this, the evolution of an American was complete. Who can doubt that if Motley had lived till now he would have approached the new and even profounder problems developed by another quarter of a century with the equipoise and the fearlessness that an American should show?

[1] Correspondence, ii. 77.   [2] *Ibid.*, ii. 193.

XXVIII

A WORLD-LITERATURE

IN Eckermann's " Conversations with Goethe " that poet is represented as having said, in January, 1827, that the time for separate national literatures had gone by. "National literature," he said, "is now a rather unmeaning phrase (*will jetzt nicht viel sagen*); the epoch of world-literature is at hand (*die Epoche der Welt-Literatur ist an der Zeit*), and each one must do what he can to hasten its approach." Then he points out that it will not be safe to select any one literature as affording a pattern or model (*musterhaft*); or that, if it is, this model must necessarily be the Greek. All the rest, he thought, must be looked at historically, we appropriating from each the best that can be employed.

If this world-literature be really the ultimate aim, it is something to know that we are at least getting so far as to interchange freely our national models. The current London litera-

ture is French in its forms and often in its
frivolity; while the French critics have lately
discovered Jane Austen, and are trying to find
in that staid and exemplary lady the founder of
the realistic school, and the precursor of Zola.
Among contemporary novelists, Mr. Howells
places the Russian first, then the Spanish; rank-
ing the English, and even the French, far lower.
He is also said, in a recent interview, to have
attributed his own style largely to the influence
of Heine. But Heine himself, in the preface
to his "Deutschland," names as his own especial
models Aristophanes, Cervantes, and Molière
— a Greek, a Spaniard, and a Frenchman.
Goethe himself thinks that we cannot comprehend Calderon without Hafiz, —

> "Nur wer Hafis liebt und kennt
> Weiss was Calderon gesungen, —"

and Fitzgerald, following this suggestion almost
literally, translated Calderon first, and then
Omàr Kháyyàm. Surely, one might infer, the
era of a world-literature must be approaching.

Yet in looking over the schedules of our
American universities, one finds as little refer-

ence to a coming world-literature as if no one
had hinted at the dream. There is an immense
increase of interest in the study of languages,
no doubt; and all this prepares for an interchange of national literatures, not for merging
them in one. The interchange is a good preliminary stage, no doubt; but the preparation
for a world-literature must surely lie in the
study of those methods of thought, those canons
of literary art, which lie at the foundation of
all literatures. The thought and its expression,
— these are the two factors which must solve
the problem; and it matters not how much we
translate — or overset, as the Germans felici-
tously say — so long as we go no deeper and
do not grasp at what all literatures have in
common. Thus in the immense range of
elective studies at Harvard University there
are twenty-one distinct courses in Greek, and
about as many in Latin, English, French, and
German; but not a single course among them
which pertains to a world-literature, or even
recognizes that these various branches have
any common trunk. The only sign that looks
in the slightest degree toward this direction is

the recent appointment of my accomplished friend, Mr. Arthur Richmond Marsh, as professor of Comparative Literature.

No study seems to me to hold less place in our universities, as a rule, than that of literature viewed in any respect as an art; all tends to the treatment of it as a department of philology on the one side, or of history on the other; and even where it is studied, and training is really given in it, it is almost always a training that begins and ends with English tradition and method. It may call itself "Rhetoric and English Composition," but the one of these subdivisions is as essentially English as the other. It not only recognizes the English language as the vehicle to be used, — which is inevitable, — but it does not go behind the English for its methods, standards, or illustrations. That there is such a thing as training in thought and literary expression, quite apart from all national limitations — this may be recognized here and there in the practice of our colleges, but very rarely in their framework and avowed method.

And, strange to say, this deficiency, if it be one, has only been increased by the increased

differentiation and specialization of our higher
institutions. Whatever the evils of the old
classical curriculum, it had at least this merit,
that it included definite instruction in the fun-
damental principles of literature as literature.
So long as young men used to read Quintilian
and Aristotle, although they may have missed
much that was more important, they retained
the conception of a literary discipline that went
behind all nationalities; that was neither ancient nor modern, but universal. I heartily
believe, for one, in the introduction of the
modern elective system; what I regret is that,
in this general breaking-up and rearranging,
the preparation for a world-literature has been
so neglected. If Goethe's view is correct, —
and who stands for the modern world if Goethe
does not? — then no one is fitted to give the
higher literary training in our colleges who has
not had some training in world-literature for
himself, who does not know something of
Calderon through knowing something of Hafiz.

And observe that Goethe himself is compelled to recognize the fact that in this world-
literature, whether we will or no, we must

recognize the exceptional position of the Greek product. In this respect "we are not confronted by a theory, but by a condition." The supremacy of the Greek in sculpture is not more unequivocal than in literature; and the two arts had this in common, that the very language of that race had the texture of marble. To treat this supremacy as something accidental, like the long theologic sway of the Hebrew and Chaldee, is to look away from a world-literature. It is as if an ambitious sculptor were to decide to improve his studio by throwing his Venus of Milo upon the ash-heap. There is no accident about art: what is great is great, and the best cannot be permanently obscured by the second best.

At the recent sessions of the "Modern Language Association," in Cambridge, Mass., although all the discussions were spirited and pointed, it seemed to me that the maturest and best talk came from those who showed that they had not been trained in the modern languages alone. The collective literature of the world is not too wide a study to afford the requisite foundation for an ultimate world-literature; and surely the nations which have brought their product to the highest external perfection need to be studied the most. It seems safe to rest on two propositions which seem irrefutable: first, that all advances towards a world-literature must be based on principles which have formed the foundation of every detached literature; and secondly, that these principles are something apart from the laws of science or invention or business, and not less worthy than these of life-long study. It was the supremely practical Napoleon Bonaparte who placed literature above science, as containing above all things the essence of human intellect. "*J'aime les sciences mathématiques et physiques; chacune d'elles est une belle application partielle de l'esprit humain; mais les lettres, c'est l'esprit humain lui-même; c'est l'éducation de l'âme.*"

INDEX

235

www.ingramcontent.com/pod-product-compliance
Lightning Source LLC
Chambersburg PA
CBHW030816020726
47499CB00006B/1942